concrete
COUNTERTOPS

concrete

COUNTERTOPS

DESIGN, FORMS, AND FINISHES
FOR THE NEW KITCHEN AND BATH

FU-TUNG CHENG

WITH ERIC OLSEN

PHOTOGRAPHY BY MATT MILLMAN

The Taunton Press

This book is dedicated to the original concrete artist:
my mother, Sung Yuan Kwan Cheng.

 The Taunton Press
Inspiration for hands-on living™

The Taunton Press, Inc., 63 South Main Street, PO Box 5506, Newtown, CT 06470-5506
e-mail: tp@taunton.com

Distributed by Publishers Group West

Cover Design: Mary McKeon
Design and Layout: Mary McKeon
Illustrator: Ron Carboni
Photographer: Matt Millman (except where noted)

Library of Congress Cataloging-in-Publication Data:
Cheng, Fu-Tung.
   Concrete countertops : design, forms, and finishes for the new kitchen and bath /
   Fu-Tung Cheng ; with Eric Olsen.
     p. cm.
   Includes index.
   ISBN 1-56158-484-3
     1. Counter tops. 2. Concrete. I. Olsen, Eric. II. Title.
TT197.5.C68 C49 2001
684.1--dc21

                                                        2001053514

Printed in the United States of America
10 9 8 7 6 5 4

The following manufacturers/names appearing in Concrete Countertops are registered trademarks or servicemarks:
The Aberdeen Group, American Concrete Institute, Aqua Mix, Betty Crocker, Brightstone, Burke, Cheng Design, Concreteworks, Corian, Durock, Elkay, Fas-n-it, Fein, Fibermesh, Fisher & Paykel, Formica, Franke, Freud, Gaggenau, Glaze 'N Seal, Hi-Tech Fibers, Hoover Color Corp., Imer, Makita, Masonite, Miele, Miracle Sealants & Abrasives Co., Multiquip, Mylar, Pfizer, Plexiglas, Quikrete, Rheobuild, Sakrete, Smooth-On, Syndecrete, 3M, Varathane, Velcro, Vise-Grip, Wyco, and X-acto.

ACKNOWLEDGMENTS

To Robert Ryan, who was there at the first countertop pour 17 years ago and went on to develop many of the techniques described in the book. To "White Blood" Wayne Battershall, "Mean Blood" Robert Bruce, "Blood" Harvey Jenkins, and Bill Guba for hanging in there with Cheng Design all these years and making it fun. To Tom Sullivan for all the mold material, no questions asked; to Julie Banfield for that crucial financial boost when we needed it most; and to Darrell Bidstrup, Chris Tong, Jud Smith, Al Jeeves, and Rob Andrews. Thanks to the entire staff past and present of Cheng Design, especially Margaret Burnett, and to the clients who so courageously allowed their homes to become our creative playgrounds. Thanks to David Hertz of Syndesis for the inspired work, and to the three other pioneer brothers of concrete work in the Bay Area: Dave Condon, Buddy Rhodes, and Mark Rogero.

Thanks to Hans Rau and H. Bates, the builders who worked on the sample kitchen. To Margaret Henry, an expert on Roman architecture and concrete; and to Andy Fadelli, concrete contractor and expert source of concrete information, who reviewed the manuscript.

To photographers Richard Barnes, Edmund Barr, Alan Weintraub, J. D. Peterson, and especially to Matt Millman for the artful images of the work and the process.

Thanks to Eric Olsen and Peter Chapman for their patience and guidance in the writing and editing, and to Jim Childs, Elissa Altman, and The Taunton Press staff for the opportunity and perseverance for this first-time author. Thanks also to Cheryl Olsen, Eric's wife, who helped get the whole project going and did a lot of background work on the history of concrete. And special thanks to Felice Matare for her selfless, inspired graphic layout models.

Loving thanks to my wife Lila and daughter An-Ya.

And finally, to Mom Cheng and my four older brothers—I'll never forget when we poured our driveway for the '54 Chevy with Mom's first concrete mix design: L.A. River sand, Redondo Beach smooth pebbles, and as little cement powder as possible. Nor will I forget the sound that driveway made when we drove over it for the first time.

—Fu-Tung Cheng

CONTENTS

INTRODUCTION

My palms sweat. A fresh-finished, curing concrete sidewalk beckons me. I sense the damp, smooth surface tempting me to leave my handprint or to scratch the initials of my first love. How many times before have I abandoned myself to the temptation and gotten away with it? I stand, poised, ready with stick in hand to scratch in her name . . . only to be thwarted by a grown-up shouting: "Hey, kid! Get away from that concrete!" I run.

▲ The author's kitchen, circa 1988. The sills are recycled redwood, the cabinets are vertical-grain Douglas fir veneer, and the backsplash is granite slate.

Years later, here I am again, tempted. There isn't a soul around. I pick up the perfect stick . . . but now no one stops me. No longer the delinquent, I can carve, scratch, stamp, mold, and grind all the concrete I can get my hands on—and play to my heart's content. Rather than being shooed away, now I'm invited to stay.

Concrete is a wondrous material. From a primal and formless slurry, it can transform itself into solid form taking on any shape. The possibilities for creative expression are endless. You can grind, polish, stamp, and stain it. You can embed objects in it. It has substance and mass, permanence and warmth. It feels earthy. It assumes forms that irrevocably touch our daily lives: bridges, highways, floors, walls, and now even countertops.

It first occurred to me to make a countertop out of concrete in 1985, when a friend and I were hired to design and renovate a professor's house in the Berkeley hills. He gave us a modest budget and announced, "This is all I can afford to spend, do whatever you want." Armed with this rare creative license, and plenty of youthful exuberance, everything was targeted to be as

▼ Recycled Douglas fir and redwood timbers, joined together with hand-cut mortise and tenons, frame the space. Concrete countertops are left and center, with a black granite counter over the black refrigerators.

▲ A skylight in the carved-plaster vent hood bathes the stove and counters in natural light.

innovative as possible. Nothing, we decided, would be "out of the box," including the kitchen sink. In fact, the sink is of special interest here since it was the first step in a process that has led to this book.

We decided to make our own sink and countertop with granite and ceramic tiles. The tiles would create a palpable sense of massiveness, we reasoned, and their complex surface texture would give the piece a comfortable, human scale. Basically, we were working toward an aesthetic that has informed much of our work since.

Rather than build a conventional grouted plywood base for the tile sink and countertop, however, my friend

and I decided to cast a concrete base. We had already done plenty of kitchen remodels by that time, and we'd seen our share of dry-rotted wood underlayments. Concrete never rots.

So we simply built a mold of two wooden boxes, one nested inside the other. We filled the gap between them with concrete out of a bag. It was a simple process that yielded quite surprising results. When we stripped the mold, we were amazed. The raw concrete was beautiful. It looked like sculpture: There was all that massiveness we liked, and the surface—gray, pitted, crazed, and textured by the mold—had all the complexity we'd envisioned . . . without the tile.

◢ The original
mold for the
author's kitchen
countertop.

▲ The author and a friend cut out the sink
knockouts after the form has been
stripped away.

▲ The first concrete behemoth weighed in
at 1,500 lb.

We agreed that it was a shame to hide the concrete, and we resolved that on our next job we'd explore concrete's potential as a medium for creative expression.

And so we did, in my own kitchen. It was a single piece containing 11 cu. ft. of concrete. It weighed nearly 1,500 lb. It took 10 of us, using two engine hoists, to turn it over once it had cured. We barely managed it, but the piece came out intact and beautiful, and to this day is still being put to good use.

It was beginner's luck, we quickly discovered.

As we designed and built more of these "working sculptures" for our clients, problems came up: efflorescence, cracks, honeycombing, more efflorescence, stains, and then more efflorescence—but each setback led to new insights and new inspirations. With each experience, we learned to simplify the process and control the variables that affect the finished product. And the more we worked with the material, the more encouraged we became.

Concrete has become my material of choice for design expression, simply because its utility and durability are matched by its sculptural sensuality. My approach to concrete is thus design driven, and this book is as much about design and art as it is about the practical aspects of working with concrete.

In *Concrete Countertops,* we discuss the tools, materials, and methods we've developed that contribute to consistently satisfactory results. And most important, we offer a gallery of design ideas culled from projects by Cheng Design and others.

It's my hope that this book will inspire more homeowners, artists, designers, architects, and concrete professionals to get their hands dirty and play. I invite you to take the techniques presented here as a springboard to explore the creative possibilities of this age-old material. I want everyone to see that concrete not only has an ancient history as a durable, lasting material but that it has proved its efficacy as a medium of aesthetic expression as well. And that today, with improvements in our understanding of its basic properties, science and industry have provided us with materials and methods that enable us to expand the potential of this amazing material.

So come on, surrender to the impulse to carve those initials.

▲ **(top and above) Good design extends the architecture from the exterior to interior spaces and carries through to the level of tactile surfaces such as the counters and the walls.**

DESIGN AND PLANNING

When most people hear the words "concrete countertop" for the first time, they are a little taken aback. They typically think of bridge abutments, foundation walls, or the ubiquitous sidewalk with its cracks, plain gray coloring, and rough texture. Maybe they even have a painful childhood memory of a knee scraped raw on a stretch of concrete. Certainly there is little in their experience to suggest that concrete might invite a touch or that it could be beautiful in itself. The inherent strength and durability of concrete have typecast it to play a structural role suitable for the outdoors or underground. We walk on it, drive on it, build our houses on it, sit on it at bus stops, and scrape our knees on it, but concrete is not really part of our intimate everyday lives. It's a bit of a leap, in other words, from that rough sidewalk to a beautiful, finished concrete countertop.

▶ The concrete countertops in this hybrid contemporary kitchen with classic overtones were cast and lightly ground.

7

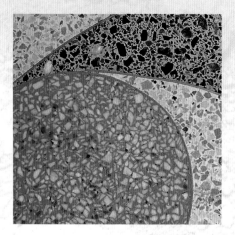

▲ Decorative inlays in concrete have a long history. Prime examples are the beautiful colored terrazzo entrances to movie theaters built in the 1930s and '40s.

Using concrete for countertops is not without historical precedent. Around the turn of the 19th century, a poured-in-place cement material called magnesite, which was ground and polished to a high sheen, was very popular with avant-garde architects such as Rudolf Schindler for use as countertops and walls. Unfortunately, magnesite fell out of favor because labor costs were high and it was made with asbestos fibers and vermiculite (which can also contain asbestos).

There's a more benign example that's been underfoot all along: the terrazzo floor. Terrazzo is an architectural process that came to the United States from Italy, reaching its zenith here in the 1930s and '40s, and is now enjoying something of a revival. You can see terrazzo outside old movie theaters or in airport concourses and city-hall lobbies: a field of colored stones or tiles against a white background.

Terrazzo concrete is usually made with white cement, with marble chips and colored aggregates. It's poured in a thin layer over a plain concrete slab, then screeded flat and smoothed. Once the concrete has cured, it's gone over with finer and finer grinding stones until it's polished to a high sheen, exposing the beautiful color and depth of the pieces of marble in a field of white.

A concrete countertop is simply a terrazzo floor raised to new heights as a working surface.

WHY CONCRETE?

The virtue of concrete is its versatility. It can be creatively adapted to any setting or any style—modern or traditional. Its hardness, strength, and mass express the timelessness of natural materials such as granite and marble. Its plasticity allows a wide range of details to be incorporated into designs, from hard-edge contemporary to ornate traditional. This versatility makes concrete universally appealing as a finish material, not just for structural applications.

And this may come as a surprise, but finished concrete feels good; it's not at all like the rough, gray, monotonous concrete we associate with brutal freeway overpasses and endless parking garages. It can be smoothed and polished to evoke the feel of worn, sensuous stone. Cast and shaped, it is reminiscent of hand-carved marble sculpture. Colored and textured, it can echo the patina of timeworn tile. Ground and polished, it can reveal a subtle, colored matrix of gradated sands and rock, such as you might find along the edge of a stream bed.

► Concrete can work in any context. Here, the earthy quality of concrete complements a traditional design.

This dramatic, sweeping bar top at a stadium pub, fabricated by Buddy Rhodes, has a hand-troweled finish.

Concrete works well in any environment, from a restaurant eating bar to a hotel bathroom to a loft dining room. It's a natural for fireplace hearths (as well as for the fireplace itself). In bathrooms, concrete can be used with stunning results as a vanity, bench, or bath surround—the sensuous shape of formed and smoothed concrete lends itself perfectly to the bathing and cleansing experience. But of all residential spaces, the kitchen offers the optimum environment where one can take advantage of concrete's unique ability to follow form—and where form can, in turn, follow function.

Concrete in the kitchen

The kitchen is the heart and hearth of the modern home. Food, fire, and water—the basics and basis of life, the foundation of human interaction since antiquity—coalesce in the kitchen. Kitchens are the focal point for family and community to gather and enjoy communion together. In our increasingly hectic and "virtual" world, there is a desire that the kitchen environment reflect and retain a sense of warmth and comfort. Materials such as stone, tile, and wood—ideal materials for the kitchen—resonate with our ancient rhythms, a tangible connection to our human condition. And concrete, applied with sense and sensitivity, can carry the same allusions to these feelings of comfort and nurturing.

▲ This fireplace surround and hearth were poured in place and treated with stamp impressions and inlays, using the same techniques for making a concrete countertop.

In the kitchen, concrete can serve a variety of functions: It can be a floor, table, room divide, bench, or windowsill. But the concrete kitchen countertop clearly has the most utility—and hence provides the most opportunity for good design to merge with pragmatic needs. The shape and slope of an integrated drainboard, for example, can become a sculptural feature on the landscape of the counter. It directs water toward the sink when it's in use and it looks great when it's not.

▲ A three-piece island with prep sink and attached dining table creates a single sculptural element in this kitchen. A perforated stainless-steel access door to the plumbing follows the form of the concrete base. The buffet and countertops flanking the stove are made of light blue concrete.

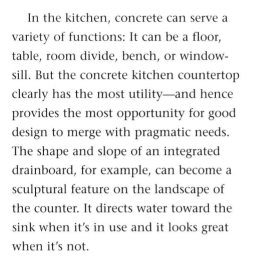

▲ Integral drainboards can be worked into a design with standard stainless-steel sinks and can double as channels for cutting boards.

◀ A cast-in-place wall becomes a partition countertop as it sweeps into the kitchen. Rather than build in a toespace, the entire piece is tapered 4 in. from top to bottom to create the same effect.

Abandon yourself to the sculptural potential of concrete: Think of it as liquid stone ready to adapt to any shape, not as just another slab material, another version of granite or Corian. Even concrete's vulnerabilities can be a spur to innovation. Take advantage of all the potential opportunities to customize your work. And have some fun while you're at it.

▲ The integrated drainboard becomes a sculptural landscape on this kitchen island.

▲ Concrete is vulnerable to staining, but a little polishing can restore the countertop to its original look.

BEFORE YOU BEGIN

There are a number of things to consider as you plan and design for concrete as a finished, functional, and aesthetic material. First, be sure you really want a concrete countertop. It's not for everyone. Ironically, just as it makes sense in terms of function to use concrete in the kitchen, this is also the location where concrete is most subject to abuse and where the material's vulnerabilities present many challenges not only to a designer's ingenuity but also, perhaps, to our tolerance for the less than perfect.

There are other considerations as well, namely concrete's mass. It is heavy. Whether or not the location you've chosen for a countertop is the appropriate one depends on the cabinetry under the countertop, the floors under the cabinets, and how easily they can be reinforced, if necessary.

Vulnerabilities

While concrete is incredibly durable, it's tough only in certain ways; it will last for centuries, but it can also stain and scratch. Unsealed concrete is especially susceptible to the many acidic liquids likely to be in use around a kitchen sink, stove, or island. Wine, lemon juice, and balsamic vinegar are particularly hard on naked concrete; if not wiped up fairly quickly, these liquids can discolor the surface or even eat into the top layer of concrete, leaving a slight roughness.

A concrete countertop, even a heavily used sink or stove run, can be kept in nearly pristine condition with the help of a professionally applied epoxy sealer or through routine maintenance with penetrating sealers and wax. But all this can take more effort than some people are willing to spend, and even then the best sealers aren't perfect. Penetrating sealers help resist stains, but they don't

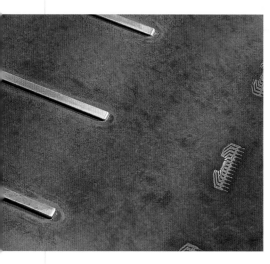

▲ Concrete is vulnerable to chipping if it's struck by a cast-iron pot. Here, brass bars make a built-in "trivet" by the stove, while copper computer-circuit parts add detail.

prevent them. And while epoxy sealers are fairly stainproof, there are problems: They scratch, you can't set hot pots on them, and they put a distance between the surface and you that reads "plastic coating." (See chapter 5 and appendix 4 for more information.)

But then no countertop material is perfect: Granite and marble also stain, stainless steel scratches easily, and Formica and Corian can be scratched or burned. Glass is fairly impermeable—it doesn't stain and it's hard to scratch—but it chips easily and it breaks. And while it's difficult, if not impossible, to

repair some of these other materials, concrete is relatively easy to fix.

Some people are bothered by concrete's vulnerabilities, or they don't like the work it can take to keep concrete looking as untouched as they might prefer. Anyone who is comfortable only with surfaces that never change—glass tabletops, for instance—or who obsesses about every little stain or scratch on the furniture probably isn't going to be happy with a concrete countertop.

But to some people, the various stains, scratches, and crazing that accumulate with the passage of time on a

▶ Given that concrete is not a good cutting surface, the integrated (but removable) cutting board becomes both a design opportunity and a problem solver.

concrete countertop aren't blemishes at all but a patina to be valued. It conveys warmth and a sense of history, like the blemishes on an antique wooden table or chair or the dents and scuffs on an old wooden floor.

Weight

Concrete is unapologetically heavy. Its mass is one reason we use it at Cheng Design, and our designs aim to explore and express concrete's heft. Thus we tend toward countertops with thicker-than-conventional front edges, for example. But concrete can push its weight around. Before sketching out the basic configurations of your countertop, it's a good idea to survey the condition of the floors and cabinetry that will support it; what you find could influence your design.

One cubic foot of concrete made with standard materials weighs about 140 lb. (Lightweight aggregates produce a lighter mix; see chapter 3, "Mix Design," for more on this.) Because a 2½-in.-thick concrete countertop weighs about 30 lb. per sq. ft., a not untypical 26-in. by 96-in. by 2½-in. countertop will weigh about 500 lb.

Most floors can accommodate this much distributed weight, especially if the countertop is to be mounted adjacent to a bearing wall. However, some reinforcing under the floor may be necessary if:

■ the countertop is very thick;

■ the countertop is part of a free-standing island in the center of a

◀ **A pastry slab of inlaid granite combines natural design and practical function: Concrete is vulnerable to the abuse of oily pastry dough and marble pastry rollers.**

room (a particular concern in seismically active areas);

■ the countertop rests on a concrete (and thus quite heavy) base;

■ the floor joists are overspanned, a common situation in old houses (if the floors are springy when walked on, the joists are probably overspanned).

If you have any doubts about the integrity of the underlying structures, and especially if you live in a seismically active area, consult a structural engineer.

There are ways to keep the weight of your countertop within reasonable limits without having to compromise

The Japanese have a concept that encompasses and defines some of the very qualities that characterize concrete: wabi-sabi. In truth, wabi-sabi is more than a mere concept—it's an aesthetic, a moral principle, a spiritual value, even a way of life. It informs Japanese arts and crafts just as Greek ideals of balance and proportion inform buildings such as the Parthenon.

Wabi-sabi derives in part from Taoist and Zen notions about simplicity, naturalness, and acceptance of reality. Leonard Koren, an architect and student of Japanese culture, explains the principles of wabi-sabi (he might as well have been talking about the principles that underlie the way we approach concrete at Cheng Design). In Wabi-Sabi for Artists, Designers, Poets & Philosophers (Stone Bridge Press, 1994), he writes:

The suggestion of natural process. Things wabi-sabi are expressions of time frozen. They are made of materials that are visibly vulnerable to the effects of weathering and human treatments.

Intimate. Things wabi-sabi . . . beckon: get close, touch, relate. They inspire a reduction of the psychic distance between one thing and another thing; between people and things.

Earthy. Things wabi-sabi . . . are usually made from materials not far removed from their original condition within, or upon, the earth and are rich in raw texture and rough tactile sensation.

Simple. Simplicity is at the core of things wabi-sabi. . . . But how do you exercise the restraint that simplicity requires without crossing over into ostentatious austerity? How do you pay attention to all the necessary details without becoming exces-

sively fussy? How do you achieve simplicity without inviting boredom? The simplicity of wabi-sabi is probably best described as the state of grace arrived at by a sober, modest, heartfelt intelligence.

▼ **Rustic simplicity at its best. Without much cabinetry, a modern kitchen by Josh Chandler instantly and gracefully looks timeless with deliberate "crudeness."**

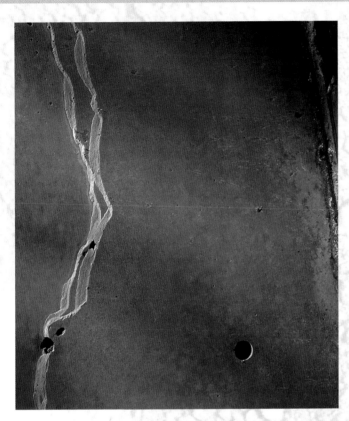

▲ The random edge of torn paper—the suggestion of natural processes—is reflected in the mold work and cast into the wall of a water sculpture.

▲ Water moves in gentle waves over a slate-and-stone inlaid channel in this countertop.

◀ A simple gesture: A small pool and rock create an intimate mood on a kitchen island with a long cutting board.

An elegant, modern version of the farm-house sink by Mark Rogero of Concrete-works. The sink, counter, and backsplash are cast to form a single piece.

your design goals. These include using a drop-down front edge, casting voids into the concrete, and working with lightweight aggregates.

The drop-down front edge

A drop-down front edge creates the appearance of mass without adding appreciably to the weight. This requires a form that is a little more complicated (see appendix 2 for design details), but it might be worth the effort, especially

if you can't or choose not to reinforce a suspect floor or old cabinets.

Voids

Some fabricators cast foam voids into the concrete to reduce the weight of thicker pieces. Voids are a little unpre-dictable, however; they can weaken the piece or cause "ghosting"—noticeable color changes on the counter's surface (see the sidebar on p. 75). Grinding and polishing can usually eliminate most of the discoloration. Foam voids can also make it more difficult to form features such as integral drains or inlays. How-ever, if you're planning a plain wall run without such features and if you intend to polish the surface, foam voids are a workable option.

Lightweight aggregates

Lightweight aggregates include pumice, expanded shale, and air-entrained glass beads. When used in place of standard aggregates, they can reduce the weight of a countertop by as much as 30 lb. per

REINFORCING CABINETS

It's a good idea to reinforce the cabinets under a concrete counter-top by doubling up side and back panels where you can (see chap-ter 6). You'll certainly want to do this if the cabinets are old built-ins without backs or if they're the off-the-shelf modular cabinets so widely available these days; the flimsy fiberboard backs on most modular cabinets will need to be beefed up.

Be aware, though, that if you add extra panels to the sides or backs, these changes can affect the fit and placement of such things as the faucet, air gap, and sink. You may also find that a thickened back panel can't be set flush with the back surface of some modulars because of the placement of assembling hard-ware. If this is the case, be aware that the thicker panels will push the cabinets forward slightly—something to take into account if you're placing your cabinets and countertop in a tightly confined

space. You'll also need to plan for some way to cover the edge of any exposed panels.

In addition, we generally recommend fastening a sheet of ¾-in. plywood on top of the cabinets; this substrate helps to stiffen the cabinets and to distribute the weight of the countertop over a greater area. Keep in mind, however, that this adds to the height of the working surface.

cu. ft. (See chapter 3 for more information on lightweight concrete.) Lightweight aggregates tend to produce concrete that's a little more porous than the standard mix, however, and lightweights are more expensive—glass beads are *much* more expensive—and harder to find.

Lightweight aggregates are trickier to control for variables that affect the finished appearance, and when exposed through grinding, they tend to produce a less interesting look than standard aggregates. We don't recommend the use of lightweight aggregates by nonprofessionals. The discussions of concrete mixes in this book, unless otherwise noted, always refer to the basic mix—at 140 lb. per cu. ft.—using standard gravel rather than lightweight concretes.

Dividing lines

We poured our first countertop in one huge piece that weighed 1,500 lb. It took 10 of us and two engine hoists to turn and maneuver it into place once it had cured. Though we all emerged from the struggle more or less unscathed—as did the countertop itself—after that project, we began to explore various solutions to the problem of weight. Now we make most of our countertops in sections, and try to keep the weight of any single section to 300 lb. or so, about as much weight as can be safely handled by two or three people.

Of course, there's something to be said for a single large piece: Its simple mass and unbroken lines can be quite beautiful. If you have the space, equipment, and labor to handle a large slab of concrete without damaging it or yourself, and if you've mastered the art

▶ **The light steel braces supporting this long, 4-in.-thick entry shelf act as a counterpoint to the massive concrete and add to the weightless effect.**

▲ An example of a seamless mold for a monolithic pour. This mold was built off-site and moved into the house, ready to accept concrete.

▲ The finished monolithic countertop, accented with a slab of marble containing fossils. A countertop this size weighs about 1,200 lb.

of mixing concrete in big batches and of properly curing a large piece, it's certainly an option.

But sectioning a countertop (typically by placing divides of aluminum or other thin material in the form; see chapter 2) does more than just produce pieces of manageable size.

First, it helps prevent cracking. Concrete tends to shrink or contract as it cures, and if it shrinks significantly, random cracks can occur. The amount of shrinkage has to do with a number of largely controllable variables, including the amount of water in the mix and the air temperature and humidity during curing; you'll learn more about these in later chapters. The mass of the piece is also a major factor in the risk of cracks. Large blocks of concrete shrink more than small sections and thus are more likely to crack, simply because there's more concrete available to shrink. That's why properly made sidewalks and other large concrete slabs contain control joints placed every few feet; these shallow grooves in the surface of the slab weaken the concrete by reducing its thickness along the line of the groove. If the concrete is going to crack, it will most likely crack along the control joint and thus remain hidden.

The second reason to make a countertop in sections is the design potential; the dividing lines between sections can add visual interest to what might otherwise be a flat, plain surface. Ideally, these lines should be diagonal or offset:

When we use terms such as "crazing" and "cracks" we're talking about two different phenomena. Cracks are the big, unsightly lines you typically see zigzagging across sidewalks and driveways. Large cracks are not only ugly but they also weaken the concrete. Fortunately, such cracks can almost always be prevented by proper mix design and curing.

Crazing refers to the network of small hairline cracks on the surface of the concrete that looks very much like the intersecting cracks in the glazing on an antique pot or the craquelure on the surface of an old oil painting. Crazing usually occurs when the surface of the concrete dries rapidly. Crazing does not affect the concrete's strength or durability. While we do everything we can to prevent large cracks, we sometimes welcome craz-

ing, depending on the effect we're after, because it adds to the visual interest of the surface. Grinding and polishing, though, will likely remove most crazing.

▼ A raku-fired teapot by Dina Angel-Wing.

▲ A gentle relief pattern on the corner of the countertop emphasizes the sculptural quality of the piece. Note the crazing on the surface.

They tend to look more intentional than straight breaks, creating a feeling that the two sections are "meant" to be together. A straight break between sections can make perfect sense if it falls along the edge of a design element such as a sink knockout or an integral drainboard.

▶ This large countertop was divided off center. The stone inlay deliberately calls attention to the division as a design element.

▶ A cast-in-place water sculpture doubles as a room divide. Every 10 sec. a small wave of water is released and travels along a copper-lined sluice to the reservoir, from which it is pumped back. The reservoir was made off-site with the same methods and technologies used for a countertop.

BREAK OUT OF THE MOLD

In our consumer culture, everything seems to come to us premade, preformed, prepackaged, and off the shelf. Thus we've become timid when it comes to expressing ourselves creatively, even in our own homes in the design of objects we use daily. Fortunately, con-

crete offers the perfect medium in which to regain some creative control over our immediate environment. Its virtues allow us to break free of many of the current design conventions that bind us, conventions that are more the byproduct of corporate economics than the result of considered or playful design. We won't go so far as to suggest (paraphrasing a principle of *wabi-sabi*)

The granite pastry slab was inserted in the mold along the diagonal divide separating two halves of the large counter. A brass rod further accents the division.

Shape and form

One way to break out of the mold is to experiment with the shape and form of the countertop. Nature rarely creates right angles, but most countertops end up rectangular because most conventional solid materials such as granite or marble are difficult or expensive to tool into more complex shapes. But concrete accommodates sensuous curves as naturally as it does hard angles, so consider curves wherever the space or function dictates the need to round off corners.

Curved shapes are especially appropriate in bathrooms, where naked bodies in confined spaces preclude sharp edges. The curving ends of a kitchen island can invite people into the space, and these curves are generally easier or

that knowing the right design solutions, one should thoughtfully offer the wrong ones, but we do suggest occasionally rowing against the current.

▲ This coffee table, made by artist Edgar Cappellin, has a steel base and a simple slab of concrete with a broken edge.

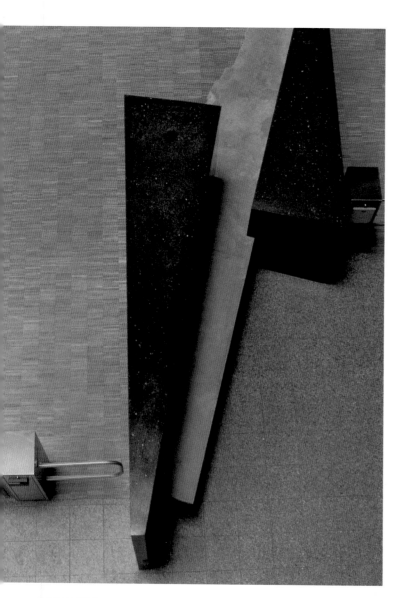

▲ A beautiful countertop, by Edgar Cappellin, made with blue-pigmented white cement creates a sculptural entry point for a lobby.

more comfortable to work around than sharp angles.

Thickness

A countertop at 36 in. or 37 in. off the floor is most comfortable for a man or woman of average height. Because most under-the-counter appliances such as dishwashers, trash compactors, and under-the-counter refrigerators are 34½ in. high, to reach a height standard of 36 in. means that most kitchen countertops are 1½ in. thick.

Cheng Design countertops tend to be at least 2½ in. thick, which provides enough material for integral drain-boards, integral cutting boards, and various inlays. Sometimes we'll do a thicker drop-down front edge—as thick as 7 in. or 8 in. Such apparent thickness is more expressive of the material's sub-stantiality and the classical look of tra-ditional stone countertops.

A 2½-in. countertop on a ¾-in. ply-wood substrate above a 34½-in. dish-washer creates a working surface of 37¾ in., about the upper limit of what's comfortable for most people. If you want to keep the working surface at

▲ A top-mounted cast-iron tub sits on a concrete precast deck and curved wall.

◀ Concrete and stone are perfect complements. The wall is flush with the slate.

37¾ in. or less but you also want a profile that's much thicker than 2½ in., you will need to put the under-the-counter appliances in a different part of the kitchen.

When possible, we'll move the appliances to an adjacent wall and mount a 1½-in.-thick countertop—typically of granite, stainless steel, zinc, or wood—above them. This accomplishes two goals: It allows us to thicken the profile

of the concrete countertop while keeping its surface at a comfortable height, and the varied countertop materials complement one another and add visual interest.

In bathrooms, you are free to some degree to design in whatever thickness suits the space and feeling of mass that you want. Vanity tops can be set from 32 in. to 36 in. off the finished floor. And cabinets can be adjusted to accom-

▲ An expressive free-form counter, by David Hertz of Syndesis for architect John Lautner, creates beautiful nonlinear boundaries.

modate the thickness of the top without having to consider an appliance. A great look is concrete mounted on steel brackets: Forgo the boxy cabinet underneath and show off the pure object in space (see the top left photo on p. 27).

Counter depth

Conventional kitchen cabinets are almost always 25 in. deep, for practical reasons: Shallower cabinets are inefficient, while things tend to get lost in the backs of drawers and on the backs of shelves in cabinets that are much deeper. Conventional kitchen countertops have been designed to match these 25-in.-deep cabinets—typically with a 1-in. overhang. Thus they're not only invariably 1½ in. thick, they're almost

▶ Concrete is the ideal material to sculpt curvilinear forms and shapes at a reasonable cost. Here, an elliptical cooking island combines a mahogany top with concrete.

The countertop fits snugly into the cast wall. Below, a perforated stainless-steel door hides the trash and recycling bins.

always 26 in. deep. But such a narrow countertop isn't efficient as a work surface, and the combination of a 26-in.-deep, 1½-in.-thick countertop sitting on top of cabinets that are almost uniformly 34 in. high tends to create a boxy look.

To loosen these proportions, you can add depth to the countertops. Thirty inches is ideal, a distance most people can reach across comfortably. This extra depth creates a more refined, less boxy look and provides more work surface. It also provides room to change the elevation of the back by adding a raised 4-in.- or 5-in.-deep shelf, a practical feature that keeps clutter off the countertop and often-used items such as spices

A large, 8-in. drop-down edge in front of the sink gives a sense of mass and weight to the countertop without sacrificing cabinet space. The edge reduces to 3 in. to accommodate a dishwasher at the other end.

Strong horizontal elements in the kitchen change the scale, relate to the horizon, and lend a sense of tranquility.

within easy reach (see the top right photo on the facing page).

The supporting cabinetry under a 30-in. countertop can remain 25 in. deep. To prevent creation of an excessive overhang, bring the cabinets forward if possible, so the countertop overhangs by 1 in. to 1½ in. Pulling the cabinets forward also creates a convenient chase for utilities such as plumbing, heating ducts, and wiring.

Beveled fronts

As the front profile of the countertop thickens, beveling back the face slightly works ergonomically and aesthetically. The beveled front with a rounded edge—typically a bullnose—yields to the body and refines the profile (see the top left photo on p. 28). The bullnose edge is a good one to have in a house with young children whose heads are about counter height. The bullnose isn't the only option, though; concrete's plasticity allows for a wide variety of edge possibilities: beveled back, eased, stepped, and sweeping. For a more traditional look, use an inset of ogee molding in the form. Generally, edges can be eased with a radius of between ¼ in. and ½ in. (anything less than about ¼-in. radius is more likely to chip than rounder edges).

Overhangs

As a general rule, let the front edge of the countertop overhang the cabinetry about 1 in. to 1½ in. When determining the overhang, take into account the placement of the sink within the cabinet. There shouldn't be more than 4 in. or 5 in. between the front edge of the counter and the front edge of the sink; any greater distance than this puts the sink too far back for comfort.

Let the edge of the sink knockout overhang an undermounted sink by about ¼ in. all around. The overhang leaves a nice reveal and creates some

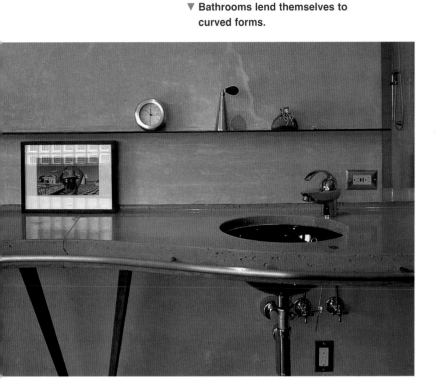

▼ Bathrooms lend themselves to curved forms.

▲ Adding a 4-in. to 5-in. raised shelf changes the proportion of the standard 25-in. countertop to 30 in., creating a more refined, less boxy look. On the practical side, the shelf helps keep clutter off the countertop.

interesting shadows. It also reduces the effective size of the sink, so take the overhang into account when deciding what size sink to purchase or to have fabricated.

Sinks

You can use most types of sinks with a concrete countertop, but we recommend a stainless-steel undermounted sink for a kitchen countertop. Stainless steel is light, durable, and looks "right" with concrete. And when the sink is undermounted, it allows for a variety of design elements that aren't possible with conventional top-mounted sinks; top mounts, for instance, eliminate the possibility of features such as integral drainboards. On the practical side, it's much easier to keep the countertop clean if the sink is mounted beneath it.

by design

The junction of two deep countertops can create a dead space in the back corner. To prevent that, consider narrowing the countertop in as it approaches the corner. This undulation is easy to create in concrete and can either curve or angle toward the corner. An alternative is to angle the countertop in toward the corner, as shown in the photo at right.

▲ A 3-in. rounded bullnose edge with sloped back.

▲ A commercial bar counter features a half bullnose corner.

▲ A 7-degree beveled edge.

Off-the-shelf undermounted stainless-steel sinks are available, but we prefer custom-made undermounts—they allow you to fit the sink to the design, not the design to the sink. If you decide to use an off-the-shelf undermount, have a specific model in mind—or better yet, the sink itself—so you know its dimensions. You'll use this information to determine the size and placement of the sink knockout and the extent of the overhangs. This information is also useful to make sure your design allows enough room between the sink's sides and the walls of the cabinet bay, for such things as faucet knockouts, plumb-ing, and the sink's mounting hardware (see chapter 2).

The design possibilities with bath-room sinks are far greater than with kitchen sinks because there are far fewer practical considerations. A vanity sink usually needs to accommodate only soap and water. A kitchen sink, on the other hand, must endure daily assaults from pots and pans, dishwater, utensils, scouring pads and cleansers, and a variety of acidic foods.

There are some very beautiful (and pricey) plain and colored glass vanity sinks available in undermount, top-mount, and exposed-bowl configura-

▲ Large overhangs are dramatic and practical. This 3-ft. cantilever is supported by a custom-made steel bracket.

▼ A top-mounted sink is the most conventional and easiest type of installation with concrete countertops, but because the edge is covered, the sense of mass of the countertop is lost.

◄ These Geocrete modular production countertops feature off-the-shelf undermount sinks by Franke (far left) and Elkay (near left).

▲ An undermounted clear blue glass sink.

▲ The surface-mounted sink evokes the simple washbasin of the past. The concrete countertop becomes the platform for the sink. This is an easy countertop to build.

▲ These double basins by Mark Rogero are integral to the top (cast monolithically) and require a sophisticated mold.

tions. Porcelain and fired-clay sinks, stainless-steel sinks, and copper and brass sinks are available and feasible to use with concrete.

In fact, the bathroom vanity is the one location we'll use concrete formed as a sink. Some manufacturers produce bowls of concrete expressly for this purpose. The vanity provides an opportunity to cast counter and sink in one piece for an integrated, sculpted look that recalls the charming stone basins of France, Spain, or Italy. Or the entire object including the stand can be treated as a pedestal sink and cast in one piece. But expect some amount of wear, erosion, and staining over time with concrete sinks, even in the bathroom.

▶ **Porcelain sinks designed for undermounting have flat rims and can be mounted to the underside of a concrete counter.**

BY THE WAY

A porcelain sink can be undermounted, but it's very heavy and if it has rounded edges it will be hard to fasten against the underside of the countertop. If you decide to use a porcelain sink, we suggest a dark color; white porcelain doesn't look as good as stainless steel against concrete.

COMPLEMENTS AND SUPPLEMENTS

Wall-to-wall concrete can be as dull as wall-to-wall carpeting, so place a countertop adjacent to other materials that provide a foil to the concrete. Also, take advantage of concrete's plasticity to create surface variety with inlays, knockouts, and penetrations.

Granite, marble, and stainless steel

Concrete goes with just about any material, but because it tends to be "active" with a variety of surface tones and textures—especially if it has inlays or if it has been ground and polished to reveal some of the aggregate—it looks best next to surfaces with more neutral colors and textures. Plain black granite, for example, is a perfect accompaniment.

▲ **Complementary surfaces work well together. Sahara gold marble and wood counters combine with a blue-gray concrete to warm up this ski lodge in Utah.**

Purists may opt to design an all-stainless or all-concrete kitchen. However dramatic, that kind of intensity can lack a sense of warmth. Instead, try to achieve a balance of drama and warmth by juggling scale and proportion and by interlacing or overlapping materials—wood and concrete, for example—at the connections. This creates a comfortable flow among materials, and in this way a visual balance can be achieved with a variety of materials.

▲ This soft green concrete pedestal and countertop is fused to a brass-plated laboratory-style sink surround with a flat slab of natural stone.

If baking is a major activity, integrate a marble rolling slab into the concrete. Stainless steel is also an excellent material to use with concrete. We'll often put a concrete sink run adjacent to a stainless-steel stove run. The two materials look natural next to each other, and the stainless steel is eminently practical—an ideal surface material to use around hot pots.

Integral drainboards

An integral drainboard that slopes to the sink is the ideal integration of form and function: It's easily formed in the mold and replicated by the concrete, it adds visual interest, and it's practical.

An integral drainboard should slope about ⅜ in. in 12 in. of run, which requires some depth in the material—one reason why our pieces tend to be at least 2½ in. thick. The drainboard can be rectangular or flared away from the sink and can feature inlays such as brass rails, which are both decorative and practical.

Inlays

Concrete wonderfully accepts a variety of materials, and how these objects are placed in the concrete can run the gamut from formal, symmetrical patterns to free-form designs. These inlays can be an expression of art, whimsy, or personal fancy. We've used pieces of automobile engines in our countertops, as well as Chinese coins, ammonites, bits of turquoise and other stone, and, in my first countertop, a Gumby embedded in the edge. Use of recycled materials is gaining popularity, espe-

◀ Richard Marks' design includes recessed wells to allow for inlaid downlighting.

▲ Green-gray counters of concrete complement the sleek, stainless-steel backsplash and countertops.

▼ Brass-rod inlays protect the integrated drainboard from heavy pots and pans while adding an additional level of detail to the overall design.

An inlay of marble was placed into a round void in the countertop.

A combination of marble, transmission gear, and bits of colored minerals were troweled into the top of this hearth. After the concrete hardened, the surface was ground and lightly polished.

cially recycled glass that has been tumbled and rounded; it's placed in wet mix, then ground and polished after the concrete has cured.

Some inlays can be practical as well as beautiful. Brass or copper rails placed in an integral drainboard—adjacent to a stove or wherever concrete gets heavy use—provide a decorative element while protecting the concrete against the insults of pots and dishes. And some "inlays" can be moved or removed. For example, we'll sometimes cast a knock-out into a countertop to hold a wooden chopping block, which can be removed for cleaning.

Of course, it's easy to get carried away and overdo it. But what is garish to one person and kitsch to another may be ironic and folksy to a third and fine art to a fourth. In any case, there are no limits to the imaginative combinations of the practical and the aesthetic in good design. Inlays are an excellent way to express yourself—and to have some fun.

◀ The beveled edge is detailed with a crystophase geode.

◀ Gumby greets the observant child on the edge of the author's kitchen countertop.

◀ Cool, understated black granite provides a foil to the earthy, purple, cantilevered concrete counter.

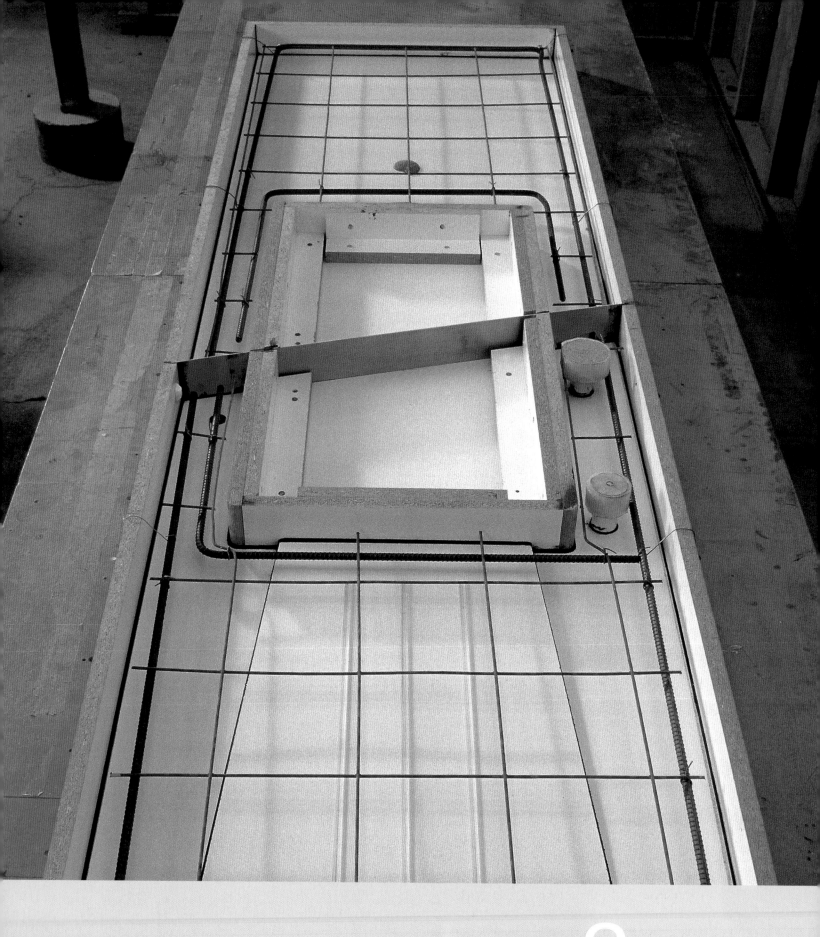

BUILDING THE MOLD

The first step in building a concrete countertop is making the mold, an endeavor that provides plenty of opportunities for creativity, demands much attention to detail, and is eminently satisfying. Molds are beautiful in themselves. They are the hidden, backstage understudies for the principal actors; they are the chrysalis from which a countertop, transformed from slurry to solid, emerges.

Most objects that are not handcrafted are created from molds. From pasta shapes and candles to power-plant dynamo flywheels and computer consoles, from spoons and forks to engine manifolds—all are pressed, poured, or cast into replicas. In order to perform their tasks, molds need to be precise.

To build good molds requires care and craftsmanship.

In this chapter, we'll take you step by step through the process of fabricating a mold for a simple but elegant rectangular kitchen countertop: an 8-ft. sink run of some sophistication that includes a few inlays plus knockouts for an undermounted sink, a faucet, a dishwasher air gap, an integral drainboard, and an integral soap dish (see the drawing on p. 38).

Almost all of the techniques used to make a mold for a complex piece are demonstrated in this project. We have included information on specialized techniques, such as curved forms and drop-down front edges, in appendices 1 and 2.

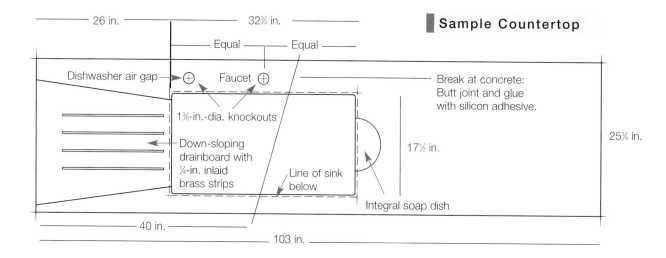

▲ Molds themselves can be objects of beauty in their own right. Above is an antique confectionary mold from Japan carved in hardwood in the shape of a resting crane.

▲ Above is an antique aluminum pudding mold from the United States.

▲ Making a mold provides plenty of opportunity for creativity but demands much attention to detail.

■ Sample Countertop

26 in.

32¾ in.

Equal

Equal

Dishwasher air gap

Faucet

Break at concrete:
Butt joint and glue
with silicon adhesive.

1⅜-in.-dia. knockouts

25¾ in.

Down-sloping
drainboard with
¼-in. inlaid
brass strips

17½ in.

Line of sink
below

Integral soap dish

40 in.

103 in.

Making a mold for a countertop doesn't require sophisticated materials or techniques, but the process can be conceptually challenging: The mold for a cast-in-mold countertop is a mirror image of the finished piece; when you construct a mold, you're essentially building what is not in the countertop. Even experienced craftsmen can have

problems now and then transferring positive design elements into their reverse in the mold. It's a process that demands clear focus on the task at hand. Any mistakes during the mold-making process will end up literally cast in stone.

The countertop featured in this chapter is part of a kitchen remodel. The

◀ Created by craftsman/artist Paco Prieto, this countertop and footrest provide a beautiful example of the sophisticated contours possible with concrete.

▲ Long sections of the footrest were cast in metal forms. The corner was created with a wood and resin form to make a double compound curve. The countertop mold was made entirely of resin-coated wood.

◀ This large island countertop has a fruit bowl and an art piece built into the top itself.

▶ These counters were poured into crude molds deliberately to make them look rustic.

MAKE A MODEL

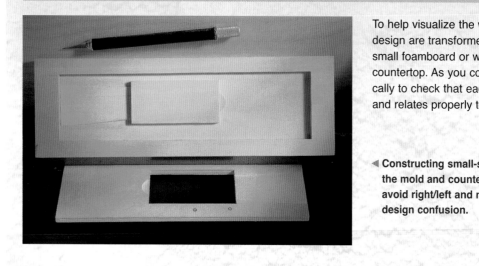

To help visualize the ways in which elements in the countertop design are transformed into their mirror images in the mold, make small foamboard or wood models of the mold and of the finished countertop. As you construct the mold, consult the models periodically to check that each feature in the mold is where it belongs and relates properly to its corresponding feature in the countertop.

◀ Constructing small-scale models of the mold and countertop helps to avoid right/left and negative/positive design confusion.

project illustrates some of the typical snags one is likely to encounter when working with existing construction, including a floor that's not level, off-the-shelf modular cabinets that need reinforcing (see chapter 6), and end walls that aren't square. We'll note potential pitfalls, where relevant, and suggest ways around them.

TOOLS AND MATERIALS

Almost all of the tools and materials mentioned in this section are available at any good building-supplies outlet. There are a few items that may be more difficult to track down, such as a rebar bender, but you should be able to rent these from your local rental agency (see Resources on p. 195 for information about suppliers); if you can't, there are workable substitutes, which are described later in this chapter. Here's what you'll need:

Template materials

The first step in building the mold is to make a template for the countertop. This template will define and shape the dimensions of the mold and thus of the finished piece. The template can be made out of any thin, stiff material, such as foamboard or thin plywood, cut into 3-in. or 4-in. strips. At Cheng Design, we prefer doorskin, the wooden sheets used to cover hollow-core doors; it's cheap and easy to use. The strips are fastened together with hot-melt glue (you'll need a glue gun and glue sticks). Keep a few small clamps on hand to hold the pieces while the glue sets, as well as some finish nails to tack the template in place while you do your layout.

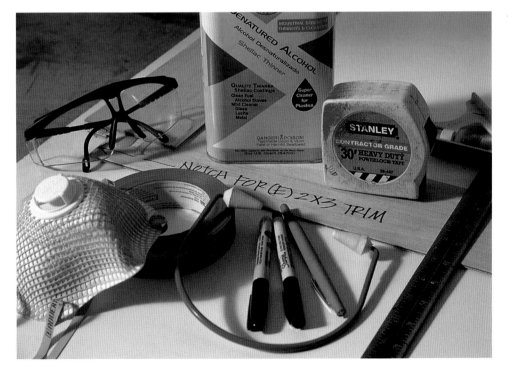

◀ Most of the tools you'll need to build a mold are readily available. Shown here are some supplies for measuring and marking— and for safety.

Mold materials

For the mold itself, use a waterproof, dimensionally stable material for the bottom and sides (there is no top on a mold); rebar and remesh to reinforce the concrete; some flat, thin material to create divides in the countertop; and perhaps a few pieces of wood and some lengths of polyvinyl chloride (PVC) pipe for the faucet and air-gap knockouts.

The bottom and sides

For the project shown here, we used ¾-in. melamine. "Melamine" is a term used generically these days to describe a number of products that consist of a resin that's glued or thermofused onto a substrate of medium-density fiber-board (MDF). Melamine comes in a variety of colors and patterns. For a mold, basic white is all you need. If it's available, use a product with laminate on both sides.

Melamine is inexpensive, holds up well, and produces a smooth, predictable surface in the concrete that requires little grinding or polishing. If you have trouble finding melamine in your area, get in touch with the American Laminators Association (see Resources on p. 195), which has a directory of manufacturers.

Divides

As noted in chapter 1, a large countertop should be divided into smaller sections. Any material will do as a separa-

▶ Strips of doorskin fastened together with hot-melt glue make an ideal material for the template. Here, measurements are being transferred from the template to a sheet of ¾-in. melamine, which serves as the bottom of the mold.

Concrete will replicate any surface, so you may want to experiment with sample molds made of materials other than melamine: glass, plastic laminate, 6-mil plastic, Mylar, and Plexiglas are all possibilities. By experimenting, you can see what effects different materials have on the surface of cured concrete. You may find something you like better than melamine; any material may work, as long as it has a waterproof surface over a dimensionally stable substrate.

▲ These samples show concrete's ability to faithfully mimic different surfaces—bubble wrap at upper left and corrugated cardboard at lower right. The lower-left sample contains ground seashells and the upper right lightweight aggregate.

▼ This period-piece coffee table mimics carved stone. It is cast concrete from an original plaster mold and clay model by artisan Dave Condon.

tor, even thin strips of wood (properly sealed against moisture), but we like to use aluminum channel. It comes in ¹⁄₁₆-in.-thick sheets, which can be cut on a table saw with a carbide-tipped blade. Aluminum reacts and bonds to concrete, so it needs to be coated with a waterproof spray sealer such as Varathane or shellac so it will release.

Voids and knockouts

A short length of 1½-in. Schedule 40 PVC pipe, slit lengthwise and wrapped with packing tape, makes a simple, economical knockout for a faucet or air gap. To create larger voids for mounting hardware, use disks of wood or MDF wrapped with a thin, resilient material such as sheet foam—the kind used for packing—so the knockout will release easily, and packing tape to seal them against moisture.

To create voids for insets such as brass rails, we typically use ⅛-in. Plexiglas, since it is waterproof and holds a nice, crisp edge. Any material will work, though, as long as it doesn't swell or distort when exposed to wet concrete.

Reinforcement

The purpose of steel reinforcing is to add tensile strength to concrete, which reduces the risk of concrete cracking or breaking when placed under a bending or twisting load, as when a houseguest decides to sit on a kitchen countertop's unsupported overhang.

For a piece such as the one shown in this chapter, which is well supported with no big overhangs, sufficient reinforcement consists of one layer of ¼-in. or ⅜-in. steel reinforcing bar (rebar) and a single layer of welded-wire reinforcement (WWR), otherwise known as remesh. Use flat sheets of remesh (the type most often used for driveways, which usually comes in 4-ft. by 7-ft. sheets); avoid rolled material because it's hard to lay in the form.

If possible, don't use rebar that's thicker than ⅜ in.: We've found that

▲ A thin strip of aluminum channel works well as a divide on a large countertop. Also visible are the rebar and remesh used to reinforce the concrete.

▲ A short length of 1½-in. PVC pipe split lengthwise and wrapped in clear packing tape makes a simple knockout for faucet and air-gap hardware.

thicker rebar increases the risk of cracking in relatively thin concrete pieces such as a countertop. For concrete that's well supported and that doesn't have any significant cantilevers, you can forgo the rebar and use two layers of 6-in. by 6-in. or 4-in. by 4-in. remesh, one lying on the other and slightly offset.

To bend the rebar, we use a simple device called a Berkeley bar bender. A bender isn't absolutely necessary, however; a couple of lengths of galvanized pipe will work as a makeshift bender for single bends; for multiple bends, use a length of pipe and a securely mounted bench vise. Whatever device you use, you'll probably need to experiment with some scraps of rebar to learn how to position the bender in relation to your marks so you get bends exactly where you want them.

To tie together the rebar and remesh, use 16-gauge soft-annealed tie wire.

To hold the rebar off the mold while you build the rebar cage, use pieces of 1-in.-thick rigid foam insulation (you'll remove the foam once the metal cage is secured in place).

Tools for cutting

Melamine and similar laminates have a hard, brittle surface that chips easily when cut, so use at least a 40-tooth blade. Better yet, use a specialty blade such as an 80-tooth laminate blade (for example, a Freud LU98) or a precision cutoff blade (Freud LU85). These blades produce a smooth cut with a minimum of splintering or chipping along the cut edge.

Try to make as many cuts as you can on a table saw. To make straight cuts with a circular saw, use a panel-cutting accessory, if possible, or a straightedge clamped to the work as a guide. Don't

BY THE WAY

When deciding how much and what type of reinforcing to use, check with an engineer if your countertop has a cantilever of more than 2 ft. or any significant unsupported spans.

◀ **To work with rebar, you'll need two tools: a Berkeley bar bender (bottom) and a bolt cutter (top).**

cut freehand, especially when cutting the pieces for the sides or big knockouts; any irregularities in the cut will transfer to the hardened concrete.

You'll also need a router with a ¾-in. roundover bit, to round edges on some knockouts or if you intend to have an upturned back edge (see the sidebar on p. 65). If you're planning an integral drainboard, use a ½-in. hogout bit. A chopsaw (with a fine-tooth blade) or a high-quality miter saw and box will also come in handy for cutting small pieces, such as the backer-board supports for the sides of the sink knockout.

There are many ways to cut the rebar and remesh. We prefer to use bolt cutters because they don't create dust or fumes. A circular saw with a metal-cutting blade or a grinder with a cutoff wheel also work well, but watch out for sparks and be sure to wear a dust mask and eye protection.

Measuring and marking instruments

You'll need an accurate tape measure, a framing square, and a straightedge for the layout. Use an extrafine "permanent" marking pen such as a Sharpie to make notes on your template and to mark the laminate. The black ink shows up clearly on white laminate and wipes off easily with alcohol.

It's also a good idea to have a 4-ft. or longer level to check the cabinets on which the countertop will be mounted. If they're badly out of level because the floor's not level, it could have an

▶ A router with a wide selection of bits comes in handy for a number of tasks when making a mold. Here, a ½-in. hogout bit is used to create a small shelf on the bottom of the mold for the integral-drainboard knockout.

◄ Filling the screw heads with plasticine modeling clay keeps the concrete out of the slots and makes it easy to unfasten the mold.

impact on decisions you make about your countertop design. Ideally, you'd level the base on which the countertop rests; if for some reason you can't, use shims to level the countertop. A drop-down front edge is a good way to hide lots of shims (see appendix 2).

Fasteners and related materials

You'll need a drill, countersink, and plenty of 1¼-in. drywall screws to fasten the mold together. Also, have on hand an ample supply of plasticine modeling clay to fill the screw heads (bright colors of clay, like red or yellow, work best because they show up well against both the mold material and the hardened concrete). The plasticine is essential; plenty of concrete will slop out of the mold and onto the screws that fasten together the mold's sides, knockouts, and backer boards. If concrete gets into the screw heads and hardens, unfastening the mold to release the countertop becomes an enormously frustrating task.

Masking, caulking, and gluing materials

Any substrate in the mold material that's exposed to wet concrete is likely to act like a sponge and pull water out of concrete that comes in contact with it. This will cause discolorations and changes in the concrete's surface texture. The substrate may also swell when it gets wet, distorting the mold. For these reasons, any raw edges inside the mold that could be in contact with wet concrete will have to be sealed.

We use spray adhesive, such as 3M Super 77, and clear packing tape. The spray adhesive helps ensure that the tape doesn't come loose during the pour. Trim excess tape with a sharp X-acto knife or razor blade. Before spraying, mask cut edges with 1½-in. 3M blue masking tape. It's not super-sticky and peels off cleanly without leaving a residue.

You'll also use the blue tape to mask seams before you caulk them—a good mold should hold water—with 100 percent silicone caulk, preferably black. Black caulk is easy to see against the

white melamine, which makes cleaning much easier (don't use white or clear caulk if you're using white melamine; it's all but invisible). Use denatured alcohol to completely clean all the excess caulk off the face of the mold.

Finally, have a fast-setting waterproof wood glue on hand if your plans call for an integral drainboard (see p. 57).

Safety equipment

You'll need the usual safety equipment you would use around any power tools: goggles (ideally with polycarbonate lenses); a paper dust mask—or better yet a respirator-type mask; and ear plugs. When using lots of solvent or when cutting rebar or remesh with a grinding wheel, which produces lots of dust and fumes, you should wear a respirator-type dust mask with a close-fitting rubber faceplate and charcoal filters. When handling solvents, wear latex or similar gloves (be aware that some people develop an allergy to latex after repeated exposure). Be sure to plug all electrical equipment into a ground-fault circuit interrupter (GFCI).

▲ Silicone caulk (preferably black) is used to seal the seams of the mold, which here are masked by blue tape.

▲ When building the mold, you'll need the standard safety equipment you'd use around any power tools: goggles, ear plugs, and a dust mask or respirator mask. Wear rubber gloves when handling solvents.

LAYING OUT THE MOLD

Layout begins with the template, which becomes the plan for the mold. A template defines the size and shape of the countertop; establishes the shape and dimensions of the space into which the countertop will fit; records odd conditions such as walls that are out of square; and becomes a sort of notebook on which to record essential information such as the location of cabinet bays, plumbing, and appliances, as well as the placement of the sinks, faucets, cabinet reinforcements, if any, and other features.

A template provides a final check on proportions and the relationships between features such as knockouts and integral drainboards. And it helps you visualize the countertop in reverse; that way you can work through your mistakes on the template before they end up set in hardened concrete.

▲ Where we started. The client's quaint old knotty-pine built-ins and less-than-quaint Formica countertop all came out. This provided an opportunity to adapt a new design to an existing space, opening up the pass-through into what had been a dining space beyond the sink, letting more light into the kitchen.

▶ Off-the-shelf modular cabinets replaced the old site-built cabinets. Though they're perfectly capable of supporting a standard Formica or Corian countertop, or even a 1½-in. marble or granite countertop, it's a good idea to reinforce the cabinets if you're planning to install a concrete countertop.

Making a template

Start with 3-in. or 4-in. strips of doorskin, cut from a full sheet. When making these cuts, keep the sides of the strips straight and parallel. Use a table saw or circular saw and panel-cutting attachment or straightedge as a saw guide.

Place one long piece onto the back of the cabinets; this piece will define the back edge of the countertop. Tack it in place temporarily with a couple of small finish nails. You'll notice in the photographs that there's a gap between the template and the back wall. The wall in this kitchen had a fairly significant bow.

Had the bow been worse, we might have scribed the template and cut it to fit snugly. Then we would have curved the form so the finished countertop fit tightly against the back wall. In this case, we didn't worry about it: The backsplash—slate over cementboard—would cover the gap.

Next, place the front piece on the cabinets, allowing it to hang over the cabinet about 1½ in. to define the countertop's finished overhang. (Remember that, for comfort, the edge of the sink knockout shouldn't be more than 4 in. or 5 in. from the front edge of the countertop.) Check that this front piece

▼ Place one long strip of doorskin onto the back of the cabinets; this piece will define the length of the countertop and its back edge.

▲ Place the front piece on the cabinets, allowing it to hang over the cabinet about 1½ in. to define the countertop's finished overhang.

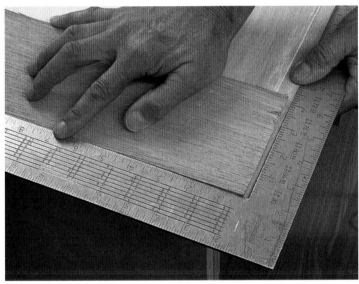

▲ Check the template for square at the open end of the countertop . . .

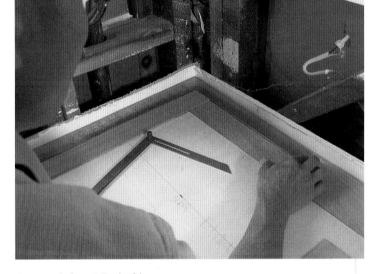

▲ . . . and also at the inside corner.

◄ Cut the end pieces slightly short, so they'll fit within the outer edges of the front and back pieces.

is parallel with the face of the cabinets. Then place the two end pieces. Cut them slightly short so they'll fit within the outer edges of the long back and front pieces. Use two crosspieces to define the sink bay.

Carefully check the template for square. The left end of this countertop was open and needed to be square.

The right end was bounded by a badly out-of-square wall. In such a situation, we'd normally re-create the wall's off angle in the template but hold the template back about ¼ in. This results in a countertop that's a little easier to install in a tight, out-of-square space. In this case, however, we held the template back 6 in. from the right-hand wall.

After installing the countertop, we filled the 6-in. gap with a small shelf made of the same slate used for the backsplash (see chapter 6).

Once all pieces have been sized and placed where they belong, glue the crosspieces to the front and back pieces using hot-melt glue. Hold each glued joint or clamp it until the glue has hardened (about 30 sec.).

Before removing the template from the cabinets, note pertinent information on it, such as the positions of the faucet and other knockouts. If you're making the mold off-site, it's a good idea to note on the template which side is the top, which edge defines the front of the countertop, and which edge defines the back. All of this may seem obvious, but we've learned the hard way that such details aren't always so clear once you've returned to the shop.

If you need to reinforce the cabinets, ideally you should do it before making the template (see chapter 6). That's because decisions you make about reinforcing can affect the placement of such things as the sink, faucet, and air-gap knockouts and the overall fit of the countertop in place. If for any reason you choose to reinforce the cabinets later, be sure to mark on the template the positions and dimensions of all reinforcing pieces that go in the cabi-

▲ Once all the pieces of the template have been sized and fitted, glue them together using hot-melt glue. Double-check the position of each glued joint to be sure it's in the proper position.

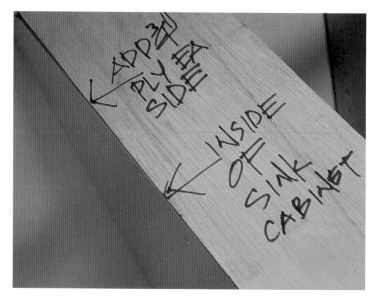

▲ Once the template is in place, note on it information such as the position of the faucet and other knockouts and site conditions such as the position of plumbing or electrical fixtures. Also mark on the template which side is the front and which is the back. This might seem obvious, but when assembling the mold—a mirror image of the finished countertop—such minor details aren't always clear.

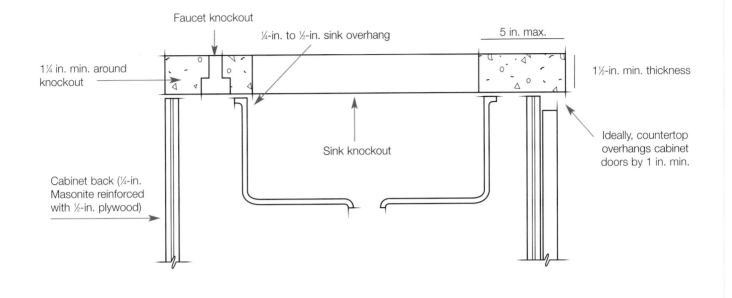

Faucet knockout

¼-in. to ½-in. sink overhang

5 in. max.

1¼ in. min. around knockout

1½-in. min. thickness

Sink knockout

Cabinet back (¼-in. Masonite reinforced with ½-in. plywood)

Ideally, countertop overhangs cabinet doors by 1 in. min.

netry. The cabinets under the piece highlighted in this chapter, for example, had sturdy enough sides, but the ¼-in. Masonite backs were a bit flimsy. We decided to reinforce these backs by laminating ½-in. plywood panels with wood glue (see p. 160). The faucet and sink knockouts needed to be positioned relative to this extra material to allow sufficient room for the mounting hardware and to be sure there was no less than 1¼ in. of concrete around the knockouts.

Using the template

Once you've built the template, the next step is to transfer the measurements to a sheet of melamine. Work on a flat, level surface and begin by flipping the template. Put it facedown on the melamine (the face of the template is the side that was up when you put the template together on the cabinets; it's the side with all your notes and marks). Flipping the template is perhaps the easiest thing to overlook. If you

◀ **The completed template defines exactly the size and shape of the mold, and thus of the finished countertop. Before you remove the template, check it once more to be sure it fits properly on the cabinets. Mistakes made at this stage are easily fixed.**

▲ **Remember to flip the template over before you use it to mark up the mold bottom.**

BY THE WAY

If you're planning to include more than one divide in your mold or if you have one that's particularly thick (more than ⅛ in.), remember to account for this in your measurements. When you remove a thick divide or several thin ones, the piece will "shrink" lengthwise (you may want this shrinkage, of course, if the piece is going into a tight space).

transfer measurements with your template faceup and make the mold accordingly, the results will be insurmountable problems, such as faucet knockouts in front of the sink.

Gently clamp the template—facedown—to the melamine, then trace the front, back, and ends of the template. Remove the template. When you make your cuts, set the blade on the inside of the lines. This helps ensure that there's enough "play" around the countertop, which will make installation in a tight space much easier. If the front edge of the countertop is to be beveled back, angle the sawblade accordingly to cut the front edge of the mold; this ensures a tight fit between the bottom of the mold and the side piece.

Make all the cuts, then put the template back (facedown, of course) and check for accuracy. Next, mark the outline of the cabinet bay in which the sink will be placed, as well as the centerline of the bay. The sink can be positioned anywhere inside the bay, as long as you:

■ remember to leave enough space between the sides of the sink and the walls of the bay for mounting the sink; and

■ remember that, for comfort, the sink knockout should be no more than 4 in. to 5 in. from the front edge of the countertop.

In this particular project, the client wanted a big sink. To make full use of the space inside the bay, we had a sink custom-made so it would fit against the bay walls. The sink's flange rests on top of the cabinet and the countertop on the flange.

On the mold, mark where the knockout for the sink bay will go. Remember that the sink knockout represents the final size of the opening over the sink. When the sink is undermounted, we always have the countertop overhang the sink by ¼ in. Therefore the sink knockout will always measure ¼ in. smaller than the sink itself. If the countertop has a divide, mark the location of it as well.

Use a framing square placed against the front edge of the mold to draw the position of the sink knockout (to ensure that these lines define a square or rectangular opening). Don't measure off either end of the mold; these ends may not be square with the front edge if they are defined by enclosing walls.

Next, transfer the location of faucet and air-gap knockouts to the melamine, again remembering to account for any reinforcing of the cabinetry that could get in the way. If you include voids for the mounting washers and nuts for the faucets and other such hardware, be sure there's at least 1¼ in. of concrete between these voids and the edges of the countertop and the sink or other knockouts.

Finally, mark the size and location of such features as the integral drainboard or cutting-board rails or stops. For this countertop, we decided on a semicircular soap dish on the right side of the sink and a flared drainboard on the left. The drainboard narrows toward the sink and has three brass-rail insets; we marked the locations of these rails on the melamine.

From the remaining form material, rip strips for the sides of the mold and for the sink knockout, being careful that the cuts are absolutely smooth and straight. Cut several additional strips of varying widths: If you decide to use backer boards, you'll need enough 3-in. or wider strips, which you can use to support the sides of the mold; you'll also need enough narrower material to back up the sink knockout. These strips are glued and screwed together to create L-shaped pieces. They can be fastened against the sides of the mold and against the knockouts to hold these pieces in place and to keep them from distorting during the pour and while the concrete cures.

We didn't use backer boards around the outside of the mold shown in this chapter; the sides didn't need the additional support. For a mold that's deeper than 2½ in., we recommend backer boards against the sides (see the top drawing on p. 65).

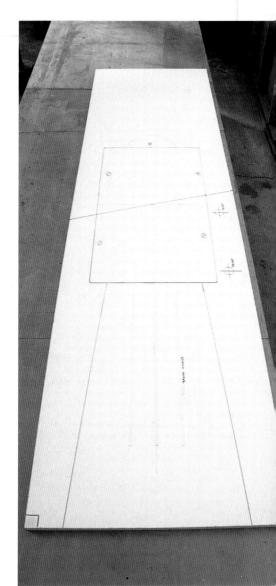

▲ The bottom of the mold, with locations marked for (from the top) a semicircular soap dish, the sink opening, divide, and flared integral drainboard.

◄ Use the template to mark on the mold bottom the location of the cabinet's sink bay; the position of the bay will determine the position of the sink knockout, the insert for the integral drainboard, and other features such as the faucet and air-gap knockouts.

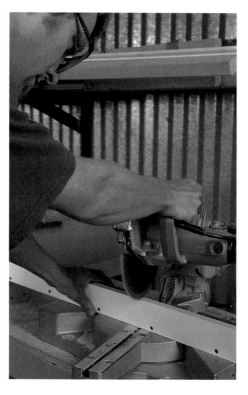

▲ ▶ Cut strips for the sides of the mold and for the sink knockout using a table saw. Melamine and similar laminates are hard, brittle, and chip easily. Use a fine-toothed blade or a specialty blade made for cutting laminate.

ASSEMBLING THE MOLD

Before putting the mold together, give some consideration to what will support it, checking for level and structural integrity. The mold will need to be perfectly level during the pour, otherwise one end of the countertop will turn out thicker than the other. This will result in a countertop surface that isn't level when the countertop is installed, a major headache at the very least. Poor support under the mold can cause even worse problems. If the table supporting the mold or the floor under the table distorts, so will the mold and thus the finished piece.

We pour most of our pieces in the shop, which has a reasonably level, solid-concrete slab floor. The molds are constructed and filled while mounted on a large table consisting of a ¾-in. plywood top on a grid of 2x4s. The ¾-in. top allows us to screw up from beneath the table into the bottom of the mold when, for whatever reason, we can't secure the mold from above. We've shimmed the legs to ensure that the table surface is as level as possible. The entire structure is more than strong enough to stay level under the weight of even the largest pieces. Now and then, however, we'll pour on-site, and sometimes we'll add temporary supports under a floor where the mold will be placed, while adding permanent supports under the location of the finished piece.

Once you've marked up the mold and cut the strips for the side pieces and sink knockout, you're ready to begin assembly. There are six basic steps involved: installing the center divide; creating the void for the integral drainboard; putting on the sides; making knockouts for the sink and plumbing fixtures; placing inlays; and assembling the reinforcing.

The center divide

Cut a kerf ³⁄₁₆ in. deep along the angled line that marks the center divide. On the table saw, use a carbide-tipped blade to cut a 2⅜-in. strip of ⅟₁₆-in.-thick aluminum. When placed in the ³⁄₁₆-in. kerf in the mold bottom, the aluminum strip should end up ⅟₁₆ in. below the 2½-in. depth of the mold. If the divide sticks above the sides of the mold and the sink box, it will cause problems as you screed and trowel what will be the underside of the countertop, making it difficult to create a flat, even surface.

Once you're sure the aluminum is at the proper height, take it out of the mold, spray it liberally with Varathane or another sealer, and put it back in place temporarily. Later, the aluminum will be seated in a bead of silicone caulk in the kerf.

The integral drainboard

In this particular countertop, the integral drainboard slopes gently down from the left to the edge of the sink knockout. Here's an easy way to create a void for such a feature.

First, prop the mold on small pieces of ¾-in. scrap so it's off the surface of the worktable. Adjust the blade of your circular saw so it cuts just through the melamine. Position a saw guide or straightedge to make a cut along the

1. To make a divide in the mold, first cut a kerf ³⁄₁₆ in. deep in the bottom of the mold.

2. Insert a 2⅜-in. strip of aluminum into the kerf.

3. Check the strip for height against a length of 2½-in. melamine. When properly seated in the kerf, the top of the aluminum strip should be ⅟₁₆ in. below the top edge of the mold sides.

1. Cut along the two lines that define the length of the drainboard.

2. Make the cut across the drainboard, being careful not to cut past the two outside lines.

5. The ledge completed.

6. Cut and glue a piece of ½-in. plywood the length of the ledge and 1 in. wider.

lines that define the length of the integral drainboard. These cuts should have a slight drift—6 degrees or 7 degrees—toward the center of the mold. This slight angle has both aesthetic and practical benefits: It puts an attractive slope on the sides of the drainboard and it makes it easy to release the mold. Make sure both cuts tilt *toward* the center of the mold.

It's okay to cut into the space for the sink knockout; this is a void in the concrete and the cuts will be covered by the sides of the knockout and their backer boards. However, when you cut across the drainboard, be very careful not to cut past the lines. Use the circular saw to cut to these lines and a jigsaw or handsaw to complete the cut.

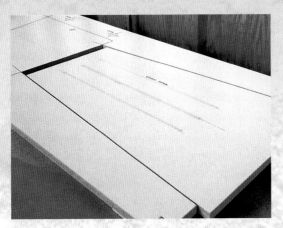

3. The three cuts completed.

4. Turn the mold over and rout out a 4-in.-wide rectangle at the narrow end of the drainboard. Set the router bit to a depth of ½ in.

7. Press the plywood into place.

8. Once the glue is dry, sand the plywood flush with the surface of the melamine (if necessary).

Turn the mold over, and on the underside, mark a 4-in.-wide rectangle at the narrow end of the integral drainboard that extends into the area defined for the sink knockout. Next, use a ½-in. hogout router bit set to a depth of exactly ½ in. to rout out the area within the lines. Use a chisel to square the corners.

Cut a piece of ½-in. plywood the length of this ledge and 1 in. wider.

Spread wood glue on the ledge and press the plywood into it. Clamp the plywood in place until the glue has set. If necessary, sand the plywood after the glue has hardened so the plywood is flush with the surface of the melamine.

Return the mold to its original face-up position. The plywood now forms a 1-in.-wide shoulder extending out from under the bottom of the mold. The narrow end of the wedge-shaped piece that defines the integral drainboard rests on this shoulder, while the other, wider end rests on the tabletop: a knockout that will create the gentle slope down to the sink. This piece will be held in place by the end piece of the mold. To keep the wedge-shaped knockout from sagging beneath the weight of the concrete—leaving a slight hump in the center of the drainboard—glue two or three tapered wood strips beneath it.

Seal the exposed substrate on the edge of the drainboard knockout by masking the face of the piece, then spraying the exposed substrate with spray adhesive. Let the adhesive dry for a minute, then apply clear packing tape. Remove the masking tape and trim the clear tape.

Finally, set your table-saw blade at a 5-degree to 7-degree angle and cut strips of ⅛-in. wood, Plexiglas, or any other material that will serve as a surrogate for the brass rails. These strips will create grooves in the concrete into which the brass rails will be glued after you've ground and polished the entire countertop. The strips should be slightly wider than the brass rails along their narrowest edge, which will define the width of the bottoms of the grooves.

Be sure to use a fine-toothed blade to cut the strips, especially if you're using Plexiglas, which chips easily. If you glue a chipped Plexiglas strip in place, the chipouts can fill with concrete fines. As you separate the knockout from the countertop once the concrete has cured,

▲ The drainboard includes an additional water channel as a feature in this countertop.

by design

Drainboards are unique opportunities to create sculpture in the countertop. They can be shaped into curves, contoured to provide drainage, or lined to add contrast. As an alluvial plain guides streams to the ocean, each manipulation in the drainboard can be a function of guiding water to the sink. It is where form follows function and where concrete faithfully follows form.

Supporting the Knockout

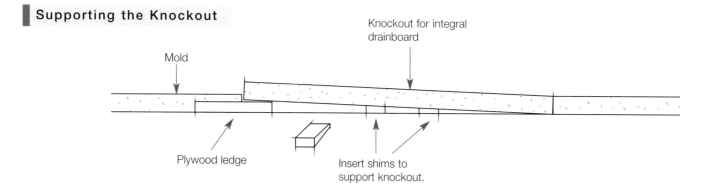

Mold

Knockout for integral drainboard

Plywood ledge

Insert shims to support knockout.

Forming Voids for the Brass Rails

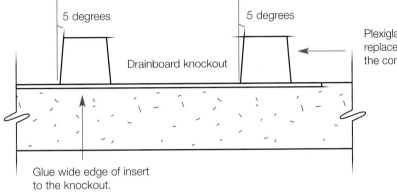

5 degrees

5 degrees

Drainboard knockout

Plexiglas inserts (to be replaced with brass once the concrete is fully cured)

Glue wide edge of insert to the knockout.

any concrete that has hardened into the chipouts may break off, creating small voids in the surface of the concrete along the edges of the grooves for the brass rods.

After you've cut the strips, check the edges. Sand off any burrs using fine sandpaper. Glue the wide edge of each strip to the bottom of the knockout. Use spray adhesive (and be sure you've glued the wide edge *down*).

The sink box

Use the outline for the sink knockout you traced on the bottom of the mold to size the box for the sink (the box fits *inside* the lines). Because the sink knockout for this particular mold was divided by the aluminum channel, the sink box had to be made with six pieces of melamine: the two end pieces and two pieces for each of the sides.

Use a chopsaw or miter saw to cut each side piece to length, angling one end on each so it fits tightly against the aluminum channel. Put the side

pieces on the mold to check the lengths, adjust if necessary, then use a roundover bit to rout a ¾-in. radius on the square end of each side piece. This curve will give the sink knockout rounded inside corners. Cut the end pieces to fit snugly between the side pieces.

The lengths of melamine that form the sink box don't attach to the bottom of the mold. Instead, they're supported and held in place by backer boards, which are fastened inside the box to the bottom of the mold and to the sides of the box with 1¼-in. drywall screws.

Assemble the backer boards from 2½-in.-wide strips using 1¼-in. drywall screws, predrilled, and spaced 8 in. to 12 in. apart. Cut the backer boards to approximate length, with the backer boards for the side pieces about ¼ in. short. When fastened in place, these won't quite touch the aluminum channel but should fit securely against the end pieces to help support the corners where the sides and ends meet.

BY THE WAY

If you notice any chips in the edges of a Plexiglas strip, you may not have to discard the strip: Glue it in place, run a fine bead of silicone caulk along the base of the strip to fill any chips, and scrape away any excess with a razor. If you miss any chips and some of the concrete breaks away when released, voids can be fixed with a slurry of cement, fines, and pigment (see chapter 5).

▲ Position the strips for the sides of the sink box on the inside of the line on the mold bottom that defines the sink knockout.

▶ Position the backer boards that will support and hold the side pieces in place; then clamp the backer boards and sides together.

Position the side pieces and their backer boards on the mold and clamp the backer boards and side pieces together. Use countersunk 1¼-in. drywall screws to attach the sides to the backer boards. Be careful not to drive the screws through the laminate. Don't screw the backer boards to the mold bottom yet.

Next, position the end pieces and backer boards and check that everything fits tightly registered and square inside the outline of the sink knockout.

Fasten the end pieces and backer boards together, then screw the backer boards with their end pieces to the mold bottom. Note that the backer boards go *inside* the sink box.

To seal the exposed substrate on the rounded ends of the side pieces, mask the face of each piece, spray the ends with spray adhesive (let it sit for a minute), then tape the ends with packing tape and trim off the excess.

Run a bead of caulk along the inside edge of the end of each side piece

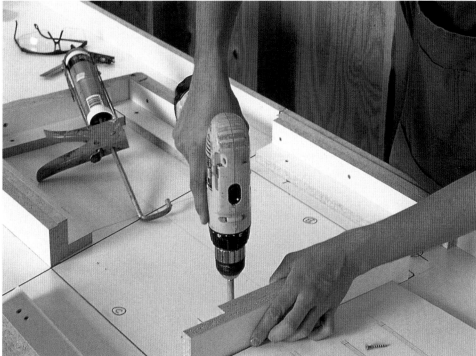

▼ After attaching the backer boards to the side and end pieces, screw the backer boards with the end pieces to the mold bottom.

where it butts against the end pieces. Screw the side pieces into place, and use alcohol to clean off any caulk that oozes out of the joints.

The sides of the mold

There are a couple ways to attach the sides to the mold. If the mold is particularly deep, we'll use backer boards for added support, screwing the sides to the

backer boards and the backer boards to the table. This not only gives extra support to prevent the sides from deflecting under the weight of the concrete, it also makes for easy release.

The mold for this countertop was relatively shallow, so we decided it didn't need backer boards. Instead, we simply attached the sides to the edge of the mold bottom with countersunk drywall

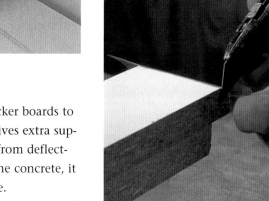

▲ To seal the exposed MDF substrate on the rounded ends of the side pieces, mask the laminate, spray the substrate with adhesive, and apply clear packing tape. Trim the excess tape with a razor.

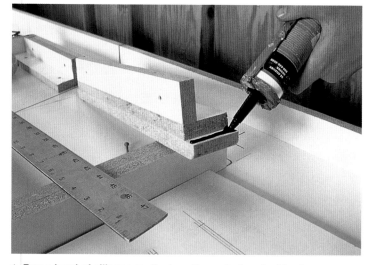

1. Run a bead of silicone caulk along the end of each side piece.

2. Press each side and end piece together and place the piece on the mold bottom.

3. Fasten the backer board to the mold bottom with counter-sunk screws.

screws spaced every 6 in. We ran a couple more screws into the sides at each corner.

Caulking the seams

The entire mold should be watertight. If any seams leak, water in the wet concrete may leach out at the site of the leak, causing discolorations and other blemishes in the finished surface.

First, mask each seam (around the bottom edges of the mold, around the sink knockout, and up each of the corners). Mask each joint with strips of tape held back about ¼ in. from either side of the seam. Run a bead of silicone

Mold Section

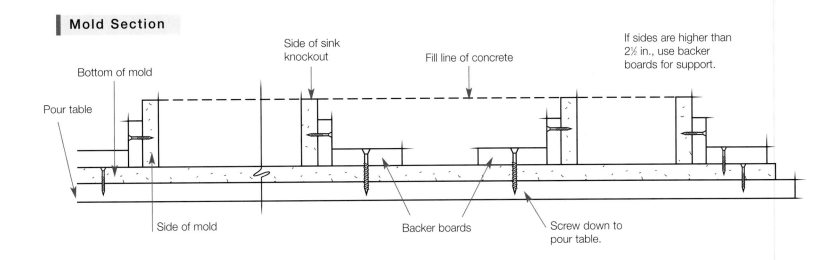

Bottom of mold

Pour table

Side of sink knockout

Fill line of concrete

If sides are higher than 2½ in., use backer boards for support.

Side of mold

Backer boards

Screw down to pour table.

FORMING AN UPTURNED BACK EDGE

An upturned back edge prevents water from leaking down behind the counter-top; it also creates a nice edge to finish to with tile or whatever goes on the backsplash.

The upturned edge is easy to form: Cut a second sheet of MDF the same length as the bottom of the mold, and ½ in. narrower (this creates an upturned edge ½ in. thick; you may want a thicker or thinner edge, depending on the material covering the backsplash).

Using a ¾-in. roundover bit, rout a curve along the length of one edge of the MDF. Spray the exposed underlay-ment with spray adhesive and cover it with packing tape.

Place this second bottom in the mold. Caulk all seams with black silicone caulk. Remember to account for this second bottom when sizing the sides of the mold.

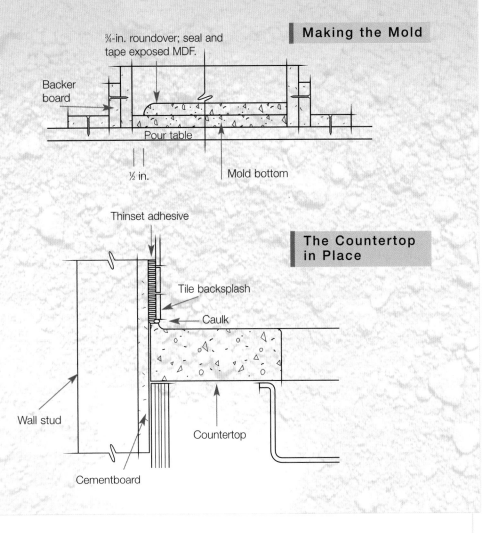

Making the Mold

¾-in. roundover; seal and tape exposed MDF.

Backer board

Pour table

½ in.

Mold bottom

The Countertop in Place

Thinset adhesive

Tile backsplash

Caulk

Wall stud

Countertop

Cementboard

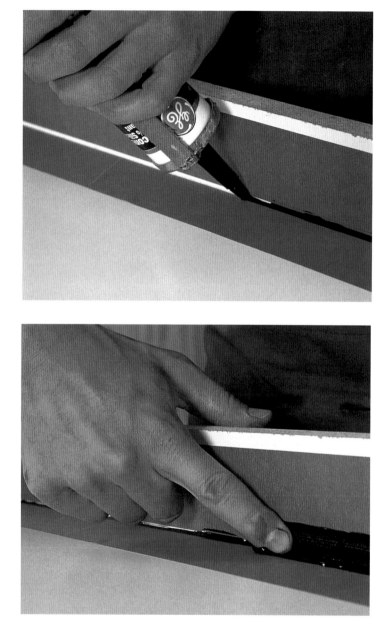

caulk along the seams, then run your finger along the caulk. This cleans out the excess and puts a nice concave curve on the caulk, which in the finished concrete will be a slightly eased edge. If you prefer a rounder edge or a tool that's a bit more precise than a fingertip, experiment with other items such as a mortar-joint striking tool or the rounded end of a wooden clay-sculpting tool. After the caulk has dried, peel off the masking tape.

To caulk around the aluminum divide, first remove the channel and mask both sides of the kerf. Run a bead of caulk into the kerf, then push the channel into the caulk. (Check that the channel goes completely into the kerf.) Use a razor blade to scrape off excess caulk, then peel off the masking tape.

Faucet and air-gap knockouts

To make knockouts for faucet and air-gap stems, start with PVC pipe, cutting a length for each knockout equal to the depth of the countertop minus the thickness of any knockouts needed to make voids for the mounting hardware. For the example shown here, each piece

▲ A good mold ought to hold water, so caulk all the seams. Mask all the seams with tape held back about ¼ in., and then run a bead of caulk along the seam. Smooth the caulk with your fingertip or any tool with a rounded tip.

1. Mask both sides of the kerf.

2. Run a bead of caulk into the kerf in the mold bottom and up the slits in the sides of the sink box.

3. Slide the aluminum strip into the kerf, making sure it's seated completely.

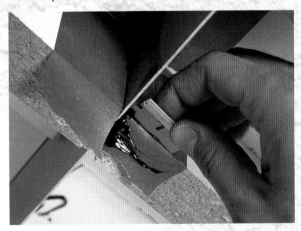

4. Scrape off excess caulk with a razor blade.

of PVC needed to be 1¾ in. (2½ in. minus ¾ in.) in length.

You'll probably need voids for the mounting hardware if your countertop is thicker than the conventional 1½ in.; almost all faucets and air gaps are designed for conventional applications, so their stems probably won't extend far enough through a thicker countertop

for the mounting washers and nuts. If possible, have the hardware on hand, so you'll know if the threaded stems are long enough, and how to size any voids for mounting hardware.

To create the voids for the mounting hardware, cut disks out of ¾-in. MDF (wood works just as well) and wrap the edges of the disks with packing foam,

BY THE WAY

Put in the knockouts for the faucet and air-gap stems after caulking the seams. They'll be in the way if you put them in first.

Sizing Voids for Mounting Hardware

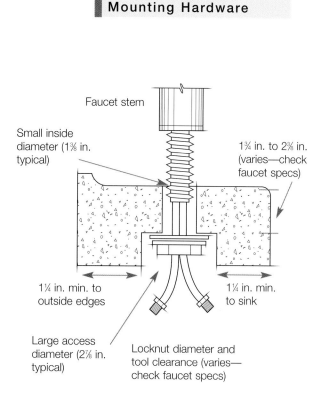

Faucet stem

Small inside diameter (1⅜ in. typical)

1¾ in. to 2⅜ in. (varies—check faucet specs)

1¼ in. min. to outside edges

1¼ in. min. to sink

Large access diameter (2⅞ in. typical)

Locknut diameter and tool clearance (varies—check faucet specs)

▲ Standard faucets or air gaps are made for 1½-in. countertop material and may not have stems long enough to extend through a thick concrete countertop. To create a knockout for mounting hardware, cut disks of plywood or other material, wrap with packing foam, and seal with spray adhesive and clear packing tape.

then wrap the foam with clear packing tape. When sizing such disks, you'll want to create a void that accommodates the mounting hardware plus any tools you'll use to tighten it. If necessary, use two ¾-in. disks, one on top of the other.

Make a single lengthwise slit in each piece of PVC, then wrap it with a thin layer of sheet foam and clear packing tape over that. The slit and foam allow the pipe to give a bit, making it easier to remove once the concrete has set up; the tape seals the slit.

If there are several penetrations close together, consider making a single large

void to accommodate the mounting hardware for all of them. And remember to make sure there will be at least 1¼ in. between any such void and the edges of the countertop and sink and other knockouts.

The disks can be fastened to the PVC and the PVC to the mold with a single long screw that passes through the disk, down the center of the pipe, and into the bottom of the mold. Countersink each screw so its head is flush with the surface of the knockout. Put a dab of plasticine on each screw head.

1. Place the hardware knock-out on top of the PVC.

2. Run a single long screw down the center of the assembly and into the bottom of the mold.

3. The top of the knockout should be even with, or slightly below, the sides of the mold.

Cleanup

Concrete faithfully reproduces any imperfections on the surface of the form, preserving these on the face of the finished piece. Even ink and handprints can leave slight discolorations on the surface of the concrete. Most blemishes won't be a big problem because they can be ground or polished out, but the cleaner the form—and thus the cleaner the surface of the finished piece—the less finish work you'll need to do.

Once you've finished assembly, thoroughly vacuum the form, then wipe it down with clean rags and acetone, rubbing alcohol, or a fiberglass cleaner to clean off any ink, caulk, or handprints. Do this once when the form is complete, just before placing any insets and the rebar, and then vacuum again immediately before placing the concrete. This is also a good time to check to make sure you've smeared each screw head with a dab of plasticine modeling clay.

Inlays

Once you've cleaned the mold, place any inlays that won't be put in—such as the brass rods—after curing. In the example shown here, the inlays were three Chinese coins, an ammonite (the fossilized shell of an extinct mollusk), and a knockout for an integral soap dish on the right-hand edge of the sink opening.

To hold the coins and fossil in place so that they wouldn't shift during the pour, we spread a paper-thin layer of black silicone caulk on the face of each piece and pressed it onto the bottom of

▲ ▶ **Thoroughly clean the mold by vacuuming any sawdust or other debris and by wiping off all marks with alcohol.**

Objets trouvés (found objects) and aged, used materials, even ancient ones such as fossils, play with time. Their resurrection into the matrix of new objects makes them resonate between the past and present, adding another dimension to our appreciation of their beauty.

At Cheng Design, we've used transmission parts, gems, fossils, and pieces of computers as inlays, as expressions of our culture and our environment. We've had clients give us personal mementos—coins, shells, stones, and the like—to place into their countertops. And we even embossed poetry into the sides of one countertop using a rubber form from a rubber-stamp maker.

Inlays provide a contrast between the concrete and these visual accents on a scale appropriate to the context. For example, a ceramic mosaic area inlaid into the concrete can enhance the subtle colors in the concrete matrix, while drawing the eye to a smaller scale of detail.

Of course, determining when a little embellishment becomes too much is a subjective call. Good design is often a matter of restraint as it is of letting loose.

▲ A rubber stamp was placed in the mold before casting.

▲ A copper bar intersects a transmission part on the surface of this concrete countertop.

the mold. Note that the caulk must be *thin;* if the layer is too thick, the inlay will be depressed into the finished surface, making the inlay appear to be sunken in the countertop instead of flush with the surface.

The caulk is sticky enough to hold the inlay in position during the pour but not so sticky that the inlay pulls out of the concrete with the mold when released from the form. You can easily clean the caulk off the inlay with alcohol.

▲ ▶ Place any flat inlays—inlays that will be flush with the surface of the countertop—before you pour the concrete. Spread a very thin layer of silicone caulk over the surface of the inlay, remove any excess with a razor, and press it against the bottom of the mold.

Sometimes, if we suspect a particular inlay might not adhere well to the concrete and there's a danger it will pull out with the mold, we'll use an epoxy glue such as PC7 to fasten a small piece of wire mesh to the back of the inlay. This mesh gives the concrete something to grip, ensuring that the inlay won't come loose.

To form the integral soap dish in the example shown here, we used scraps of a Formica countertop cut into two circles, one with a diameter ¼ in. smaller than the other. We cut the circles in half and sanded the larger piece so it was thicker along the flat edge than along the curved edge (¾ in. narrowing to a bit less than ½ in.). This puts a gradual slope in the integral soap dish down toward the sink knockout. As an added relief, we inserted a small, flat piece of ¼-in. scrap against the sink knockout and the two disks against that. All three pieces were glued together and to the mold with black silicone caulk. We sealed all raw edges with spray adhesive and packing tape.

Forming the Soap-Dish Insert

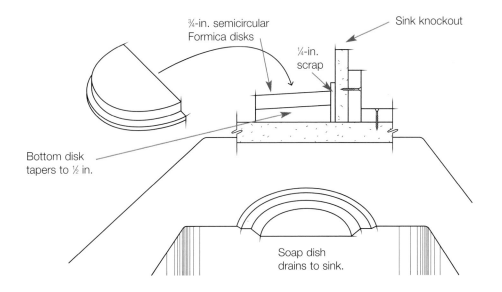

¾-in. semicircular Formica disks

¼-in. scrap

Sink knockout

Bottom disk tapers to ½ in.

Soap dish drains to sink.

Reinforcement

Some fabricators rely on fibers to reinforce the concrete (see pp. 91–92). We usually use fibers along with ¼-in. or ⅜-in. rebar and a layer of remesh. In the piece shown here, we placed a single layer of rebar around the outside edge of the countertop and another around the sink knockout, then tied a sheet of remesh onto the rebar.

We used our template to size the rebar and position the bends so that:

- no length of rebar is within 1½ in. of the edges of the countertop or any knockouts, and

- no rebar end is within 1½ in. of the divide or any knockout.

◀ You can form details like this integral soap dish with scraps of MDF or Formica, held in place with silicone caulk.

> The best way to bend rebar is with a simple tool called a Berkeley bar bender. A length of pipe and bench vise can also serve as a makeshift bender.

We marked the position of the bends in the rebar with masking tape and used a bender to make precise, 90-degree bends, checking each bend for square before making the next.

We bent two pieces of rebar and placed them on either side of the aluminum divide. One "U" on each side wrapped around the outside edge of the mold. Another, smaller "U" wrapped around the sides of the sink knockout opposite the faucet and air-gap knockouts. On the side with the knockouts, an L-shaped piece of rebar wrapped around two sides of the sink box.

Rebar should be placed at least 1 in. above the bottom of the mold (that is, what will be the face of the finished countertop). Use pieces of 1-in. foam insulation to hold the rebar off the bot-

tom of the mold (these pieces of foam will also help protect the mold from scratches as you place the rebar to check fit and position).

You may want to use more rebar if there's not going to be much support under your countertop or if it has a big overhang that is likely to come under such loads as bags of groceries or someone's posterior. In such cases:

- Lay a network of rebar on 1-ft. or 6-in. centers, with a layer of remesh on top.

- For a piece that's more than 3 in. thick, consider two layers of rebar, one above the other, perhaps slightly offset, and separated by at least ¾ in. Concrete may not flow around pieces of rebar that have been placed

◀ Temporarily place the rebar on pieces of 1-in. foam insulation. This helps protect the melamine from scratches and holds the rebar off the mold bottom the correct distance.

too closely together, which could create voids and weaken the piece. This is especially true if the concrete has been mixed with the least amount of water, has begun to stiffen a bit before being poured, or is not completely vibrated. And again, neither layer of rebar should be placed within 1 in. of either surface (top or bottom).

▥ For an unsupported overhang, run two or three pieces of rebar from the main body of the piece into the cantilevered section and along its outer edge, again keeping the rebar back 1½ in. from the edge. Also, keep all parallel rebar at least ¾ in. apart. As a rule of thumb, no more than one-third of the uninterrupted

length of the countertop—and the rebar in it—should be unsupported, but again, we recommend checking with an engineer about the best way to reinforce or support any significant overhangs.

Once you've made the bends, carefully place each piece of rebar in the mold to check for size and position. Remember, the rebar should be no closer than 1½ in. to the sides of the mold or sink knockout. When you're satisfied that the rebar is in the right position, lay a sheet of remesh over the mold and use masking tape to mark the position of the cuts. The trimmed remesh will lie flat on the rebar.

BY THE WAY

When splicing pieces of rebar, avoid lap splices (when two ends overlap). Such splices are all right when reinforcing slabs poured on the ground, but like rebar that's too big, lap splices seem to increase the risk of cracks. When available, use rebar that is long enough to span the entire length of a piece, so you can avoid having to make lap splices.

GHOSTING

If rebar is placed less than 1 in. from the surface of the concrete, it increases the risk of cracking or visible "ghosting," a slight discoloration on the surface directly above the rebar. This ghosting can usually be polished out, but it's best to avoid it if possible. If rebar passes over a sloping piece such as the knockout for an integral drainboard, you may need to adjust its position so it clears the knockout by at least 1½ in. Where two pieces of rebar join in such a situation, rather than overlap them, butt one piece to the other and fasten with wire.

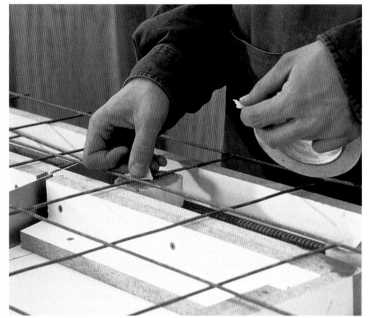

▲ Once the rebar
is in place, lay
a sheet of remesh
on the mold
and mark cuts
with tape.

BY THE WAY

Don't wrap the supporting wires around the rebar. A hook allows for the easy removal of the cage if you find you need to take it out again—perhaps because you've forgotten an inlay or because you find the mold still needs one more thorough cleaning before you pour the concrete.

Cut the remesh with bolt cutters, heavy-duty wire cutters, or a cutoff wheel (watch the sparks). Place it carefully into the mold. Use tie wire to fasten the remesh to the rebar. You need just enough ties to keep the rebar and remesh cage in position as you pour and vibrate the concrete—say, one tie about every 8 in. to 12 in. At this point, the cage can still be easily lifted out of the mold in one piece, and it's not a bad idea to remove the cage and give the mold a second vacuuming; once the cage is hung in place, the mold will be difficult to clean.

To hang the cage, place screws around the outside of the mold every 12 in. or so (be careful not to screw through the form material). Wrap a piece of tie wire around the screw and loop it over the side of the mold, mak-

ing a hook to catch the rebar at the other end. Once the cage is hung, don't forget to remove the pieces of insulation. After you pour the concrete, you'll snip off the hooks below the surface of the wet concrete.

Final touches

Before you're about to pour the concrete into the mold, fasten the mold to the table, first making sure the table is level and that the tabletop is free of debris. Fastening the mold to the table is very important: If the mold is racked even slightly, the finished piece that comes out of the mold will also be racked and very hard to level during installation. Screwing the mold to the table will flatten any twists and keep the mold securely in place during the pour.

◀ Use tie wire to fasten the remesh and rebar together. Then hang the cage from tie-wire hooks fastened to the exterior of the form. Don't forget to remove the foam insulation.

To secure the mold, toenail 1¼-in. drywall screws into the tabletop every 8 in. around the outside edge of the mold (predrill the holes first). Also run four screws (one in each corner) through the bottom of the mold in the sink knockout.

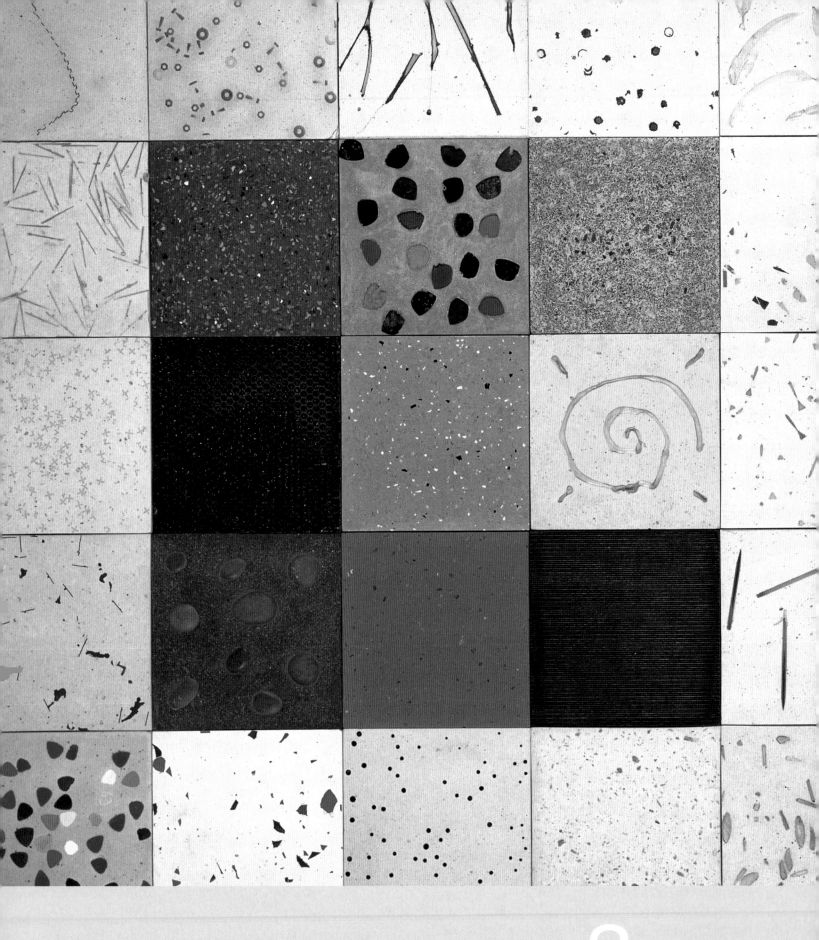

CHAPTER 3

MIX DESIGN

Making concrete is a bit like baking a cake; you don't need a lot of fancy equipment, tools, or materials to achieve pleasing results. To bake a cake, you might choose to buy a box of mix at the grocer, add water, stir, then pour the batter into a mold and insert it into a preheated oven. And you'd get credible results. But creative souls, not content to simply stir and bake, will begin to experiment—adding nuts and raisins perhaps, or maybe extra chocolate chips. Then, emboldened by the results, they may decide to dispense with the mixes entirely and turn to fresh ingredients and sophisticated recipes, discovering new dessert delights. The variations and creative possibilities become endless; the leap from Betty Crocker to sophisticated French pâtisserie is a leap of faith and imagination.

Leftover concrete, of course, can't be consumed the next day, so we must be careful not to stretch the analogy too far. But with concrete, as with cake, you can simply toss together your ingredients—some gravel, sand, and cement, or bagged readymix available at your local hardware store—add water until the mix looks about right, hoe for a while in a wheelbarrow, and then dump it all into a mold. Chances are fairly good that you'll end up with a workable, fine-looking piece.

At Cheng Design, we have worked up some recipes of our own that make the leap to "French pâtisserie," and a basic recipe from our repertoire is included in this chapter. It's one we've

Eons ago, Mother Nature created her own tectonic mix design with mud and silt, entombing minerals and shells under glacial vises and heating them in magma kilns to create vast deposits of rock and limestone. Today, we quarry these dormant treasures and process them into beautiful polished slabs of variegated granites and marbles to embellish our buildings and houses.

The concrete mix design we use at Cheng Design mimics and compresses this natural process into a 10-day event. With the raw materials from nature—graded aggregates and sands and pulverized minerals—we create our own compositions of pattern and color. Fossils, laid into the matrix of concrete, echo what Mother Nature began. Ground and polished, the hardened surface of our concrete mix reveals the natural aggregate of sand and stones. In this way, we create understated references to nature while celebrating the hand of man.

▲ **A translucent natural crystal accents a corner of a counter.**

▶ **A 250-million-year-old pyritized ammonite fossil slice is reinserted into a matrix of a concrete countertop.**

devised through trial and (a bit of) error, and find to be a useful architectural concrete mix that gives consistently good results. We first designed the mix for countertops, but it's equally appropriate for floors, room dividers, and any other application in which the look of the concrete's finished surface is paramount.

We describe this mix in this chapter and provide a precise formula for it. We offer it for those of you who like plenty of creative and technical control over the results of your endeavors, and we suggest you think of this mix as a starting point. You might try different mixes, using a variety of ingredients in varying proportions. You may find a mix that suits your needs or aesthetics much better than the mix outlined here. Also, bagged concrete and readymix—concrete that is delivered to the site in a transit mixer—are options, and both have advantages and disadvantages, which we'll discuss later in this chapter.

THE BASICS

As a concept, concrete is probably at least as old as *Homo sapiens*. Man, it seems, has been trying to stick things together with mud—the earliest concrete, if you will—since there was Man.

Of course, mud has one obvious and serious flaw as a building material: It dissolves in the rain. It's not entirely clear when our ancestors first solved that problem. We do know that the

Egyptians used burnt gypsum mortar to bind together the stones in the pyramids and that the Mesopotamian cultures used clay—a sort of high-tech mud—and sun-dried and burned bricks to produce fairly durable structures.

The first concrete

The first real concrete was probably developed during the Bronze Age (around 1600 B.C.) by the Greeks, when they began combining fine volcanic ash, lime, and sand to produce a rudimentary but tough mortar.

By the 4th century B.C., the Romans were producing a cement that contained slaked lime and a singular type of volcanic ash found around the town

▲ The so-called Temple of Minerva Medica in Rome was built in the 3rd century B.C. Like many Roman concrete structures, it was built on a wooden framework. The structure's tile facing was laid on the framework, and the concrete was poured onto the tile. When the wooden forms were removed, the tile remained cemented in place.

◄ The concrete arches in Palestrina were poured around 100 B.C. They had a tufa revetment, or facing, and were probably poured on wooden forms. Very often in this type of construction, the stone facing would be covered with a coating of stucco.

of Pozzouli (thus the name of today's admixture, pozzolan) at the base of Mt. Vesuvius. This cement is probably the world's first true "hydraulic" cement: a cement that will harden under water.

While they were refining their cements, the Romans also advanced the art and science of using aggregates. A look at examples of hundreds of samples of Roman architecture suggests that sand and coarse aggregates were graded for size and were specially screened, just as aggregates are today. And the Romans' use of uniformly sized aggregates appropriate to their position in a building—large rocks in foundations; smaller pieces, pottery shards, and broken bricks in walls; and lightweight aggregates, including pumice, in vaults—set the standard for building with concrete until 1824. That's when Joseph Aspdin, a bricklayer in Leeds, England, patented a cement he named after the limestone quarried near Portland, England. There have been many improvements on Aspdin's original mix in the years since, but essentially what he concocted nearly 200 years ago is the cement we use today.

Portland cement

Modern portland cement is a carefully proportioned mix of quite ordinary materials—lime, or calcium carbonate, from limestone, chalk, or even seashells; silica from sand or shale; and iron oxides from iron ore or maybe a bit of furnace slag or mill scale—that are transformed by heat into something that works in ways no one has yet fully explained.

The transformation from the mundane to the mysterious begins when the various raw materials are mixed together in specific proportions—lime and silica make up 85 percent of ingredients—crushed into a course powder, then heated in a kiln for several hours at 2,700°F. As the mix heats, carbon dioxide, water, and several other compounds are driven off and the various minerals in the mix fuse to form entirely new compounds, which emerge from the kiln in walnut-sized, rocklike lumps called clinkers. These clinkers are then ground into an extremely fine powder (about 150 billion grains in a pound of cement) and mixed with a small amount of gypsum to regulate setting time, plus other additives, depending on the qualities desired, to become what we commonly call cement.

Technically speaking, however, this powder isn't cement until water is added, beginning a reaction called hydration. Hydration is not a process of drying out; in fact if the concrete dries out, hydration will stop. Rather, hydration involves the formation of completely new compounds, crystalline structures of incredible intricacy that bond to one another and to whatever is mixed in with them—to the sand, gravel, and rebar, for example.

It's the crystalline structure of this cement that gives concrete its strength and durability—and ultimately its appearance—but pure cement by itself is brittle. Most of concrete's strength develops from the formation of bonds not between the crystals themselves but between these crystals and the aggre-

BY THE WAY

Tremendous amounts of energy are used to manufacture the portland-cement powder that is in concrete. Although relatively inexpensive to buy and easy to obtain the world over, there is good reason not to squander this resource. If we as architects, designers, builders, and homeowners can pause and treat our next project in concrete with the same reverence and respect as a sculptor pausing before carving into a chunk of flawless marble, then perhaps we can leave an enduring legacy of our joy in the creative process while practicing the highest form of environmental responsibility: conservation.

gates and reinforcing materials, locking them all together into a dense, durable material that can last for centuries.

A host of factors can affect the integrity of these bonds, and much of what goes on when mixing, pouring, and curing concrete is intended to foster their development or to prevent them from breaking.

During the first few hours after hydration, cement generates heat and expands slightly, then it cools to the ambient temperature and continues to cure and harden. Concrete hardens rapidly during the first few days after it's placed, and it gains about two-thirds of its strength in the first 4 weeks. It gains roughly another 50 percent in strength in the following 5 months and continues to gain strength slowly for decades after. During the first few days after hydration, "green" concrete that's not properly mixed or cured may shrink, and as it shrinks, some of the bonds between the cement, the aggregates, and the rebar may break, causing cracks and weakening the concrete.

Types of portland cement

There are many types of portland cement, some designed for specific applications, some for economy. The most common is Type I cement. It's comparatively cheap, so it's often used on big jobs, but it tends to generate a lot of heat during the early stages of curing and then shrink and crack more than other types. Thus it's useful for such applications as sidewalks, driveways, and retaining walls but not for countertops or other architectural pieces in which appearance and finish are important.

If you order readymix, you might get Type I unless you specify otherwise, so

THE IDEAL MIX

The most important thing to keep in mind when mixing concrete is that the least amount of water used in relation to the cement produces the least amount of shrinkage and the strongest, most durable concrete. Moreover, by keeping the water content of the mix low, you reduce the risk of blemishes such as water stains and efflorescence (see chapter 5 for more on this). The ideal mix, in fact, would have just enough water to thoroughly hydrate the cement and not a drop more. But such concrete is almost impossible to work because it's too stiff.

When adding water to concrete, then, you're always making compromises between maximum strength and adequate workability. By being careful with the addition of water and by using admixtures such as a water reducer, it's possible to produce workable concrete that won't shrink when cured and is very strong.

Other factors that affect the strength of concrete include the size and type of aggregate used in the mix, how well the ingredients are blended, how thoroughly the concrete is vibrated after it's poured, whether or not the concrete is disturbed in the first few days after the pour, and the environmental conditions during the curing process.

be sure to ask (depending on the batch plant, Type I may be all that's available). Type IV and Type V cements, as well as a variety of blended cements, are for specialized applications and we won't consider them here.

When it comes to concrete countertops or similar pieces, we need to concern ourselves with only three kinds of cement: Type II and Type III cements and white cement.

■ **Type II cement** is more suitable than Type I cement for pieces such as countertops, in which finished appearance is important; it's less prone than Type I to shrinkage or cracking. Concrete made with Type II cement gains strength more slowly than concrete made with Type III cement, however, and it ought to be kept undisturbed in the form for at least 7 days after the pour. This can be inconvenient if you're pouring on-site or in a busy shop and have to work around the piece.

■ **Type III cement,** also known as "high-early" cement, sets up at about the same rate as Type II cement, but it gains strength much more quickly. At 3 days, for instance, concrete made with Type III cement is as strong as concrete made with Type II cement at 7 days; at 1 week, it's as strong as Type II cement at 28 days. At 28 days, however, concretes made with Type II or Type III cements are about equal in strength; Type III just achieves that strength more quickly.

Type III cement is a good choice if you're pouring on-site or in a busy setting, because pieces made with it can be broken out of the mold and moved out of the way 3 days or 4 days after a pour. Type III is also a good choice if you're working in very cold or very hot, dry conditions, since you don't have to control the curing environment for more than 4 days, after which time the concrete will be more or less impervious to temperature extremes or low humid-

SETTING, CURING, AND HARDENING: A Few Definitions

You'll encounter terms such as "setting time," "curing," and "hardening time" in this and other discussions about concrete. These terms refer to somewhat different things. The setting time of concrete is the time it takes for concrete paste to lose its plasticity and begin to harden—or, in the parlance of those on the job, to "go off." That might be a matter of minutes or hours, depending on the air temperature, humidity, and how much the concrete is agitated;

concrete left undisturbed will set up more quickly than concrete that's being mixed.

Curing refers to the deliberate process, usually lasting a few days or a week after a pour, of controlling the temperature and humidity of the environment around "green" concrete to facilitate hardening and prevent shrinkage, cracking, and other problems. Concrete cures rapidly during the first 28 days after it has been poured and then continues to harden slowly for years.

▲ Type III cement is a good choice if you're pouring on-site or if you're working in very cold or very hot, dry conditions.

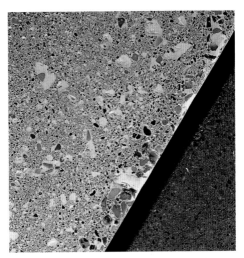

▲ White cement is made without iron oxides. It yields a concrete that's lighter in tone than concrete made with gray cement. Pigments mixed into concrete made with white cement tend to produce brighter but less natural-looking colors.

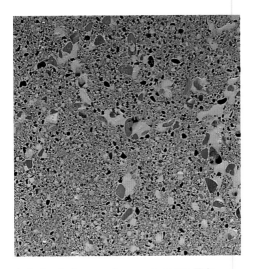

▲ A simple terrazzo is easy to make. This sample was produced using white cement and pieces of turquoise and jadeite mixed in with the sand and gravel. The piece was not vibrated after placing the concrete, which allowed air bubbles to form, creating voids in the surface. After the piece cured, the holes were filled with a slurry of white cement, fines, and water. The surface was lightly ground and polished to reveal the aggregates.

ity. Type II needs to be protected from such extremes for about a week.

▪ **White cement** is cement that's been made without iron, so it is, as the name says, white. Otherwise, it has the same basic characteristics as Type II cement. White cement is typically used with pigments when bright or light colors are desired. If you use white cement, you'll need to be careful in selecting light-colored sand because dark sands will dull the colors. The color of the aggregates won't matter significantly, although expanded shale, a common lightweight aggregate, is brown and will tend to warm up any color you use.

Also, be sure that your aggregates are clean; dirty aggregates can also dull the color.

If you grind and polish the piece after it has cured, be aware that this can affect the color in a couple of ways: First, it will remove some of the most intensely colored "cream" (the fine layer of cement on the surface of the concrete) and will tend to dilute and dull the color. Second, exposing the aggregate will change the color in ways that depend on the color of the aggregate itself.

Whether you're planning to use white cement or gray Type II or Type III cements, if your goal is a specific quality

BY THE WAY

There can be subtle differences between the gray tones of concrete made with Type II cement and concrete made with Type III cement. The differences are slight, but if you're trying to match the color of concrete from a previous pour—never an easy task under any circumstances—or if you're mixing several batches for one pour, be sure to use the same type of cement (and the same brand, if possible).

▲ Color intensity is not a problem with a white-cement mix, as shown by these round concrete-topped tables by Syndesis.

▶ Chromium green and yellow oxide in white cement. The "pinstripe" line is created in the mold with a line of silicone caulk.

of color, it's always a good idea to make some test panels first using available sand and aggregates, the desired mix of pigments, and a variety of sealers. This way you'll be able to see what the finished color will actually be (see the sidebar on the facing page).

Sand and aggregates

The nature of the aggregates used also plays a role in concrete's strength—and in its finished appearance. An even continuum of aggregate sizes from the finest (sand, or "fines") to the coarsest (gravel) produces the strongest concrete when the maximum size of the aggregates (MSA) used is no more than about ⅜ in. in diameter. Such a mix of aggregates provides the maximum surface area for strong bonds to form between cement, sand, and gravel.

When larger gravel is used, or when there's little variation in size between the smallest and largest pieces, pockets of hydrated cement are more likely to form in the gaps between the pieces of aggregate. These pockets will tend to shrink, pulling away from the surrounding aggregate and causing cracks. (Such fragile pockets are also more likely to form if the concrete is inadequately mixed or vibrated.)

Common aggregates are made from crushed rock or natural gravel dug out of local stream beds and alluvial fans. These produce concrete that weighs about 140 lb. per cu. ft. Lightweight aggregates, which produce concrete that weighs about 110 lb. per cu. ft., come from a variety of sources: If there happens to be a volcano nearby (or at least the remnants of one), pumice, volcanic

▲ ▼ **Make a half dozen or more small samples to experiment with pigment recipes or to test the effects of grinding and polishing, as well as different types of sealers.**

If you're pouring a countertop for the first time or if you're using bagged concrete, we recommend that you make some samples in advance. Use some samples to test different pigment concentrations and the effects of local materials on the finished color. Use others to test different grinding and polishing techniques and to test the effects of different sealers and waxes on the appearance of the finished countertop.

Making the form

To make a form for the samples, use the same material you plan to use for the main piece (in this case, MDF with melamine laminate). To make six small samples, start with a 2-ft. by 4-ft. sheet of MDF and enough 1-in.- or 2-in.-wide strips of MDF for a border and divides, as shown in the photo above.

Cut the strips to size so they can be positioned to divide the sheet into six 12-in. by 16-in. rectangles. Seal the exposed substrate on these strips with spray adhesive and packing tape (see chapter 2). Fasten the strips to the sheet using drywall screws, and put a dab of plasticine modeling clay on each screw head.

During the cure

As the concrete sets up in the sample mold, note how much it pulls away from the sides. Any concrete will pull away slightly, and a paper-thin gap between the concrete and the sides of the mold is acceptable. A gap that's wider indicates that the mix was probably too wet or, if you used bagged mix, the ingredients were of low quality. In either case, lots of shrinkage indicates that the concrete is likely to crack.

The color of concrete tends to change as it cures and ages; to get the best indication of the finished color, make your samples well ahead of the actual pour—about 3 weeks or 4 weeks, ideally. Cure the samples as you would the finished piece, under the same conditions.

Testing the samples

Grind some samples to see the effect on the color. Grinding tends to lighten the intensity of colors by removing some of the highly pigmented cream. On the other hand, grinding can darken the piece by exposing aggregate.

To gauge the effect of sealers on color, apply a few different types— penetrating sealers and epoxies—to the samples, and experiment with waxes over the sealers, which tend to darken colors. (See chapter 5 for more on curing, grinding, and sealing.)

If you're working near the
ocean, fight the quite natural
temptation to use beach sand
or gravel in your mix; the salt on
the sand and gravel will ruin the
concrete. Similarly, use only clean
fresh water, never saltwater or
muddy water.

scoria, or porous lava might be available. Manufactured lightweight aggregates include expanded shale, clay, slate, and expanded glass beads.

Which type of aggregate is best? For the project highlighted in this book—a countertop that we ground and polished—we used natural gravel. Natural gravel has several advantages over crushed rock and lightweight aggregates:

- Natural gravel has a more interesting appearance when exposed through grinding than either crushed rock or lightweight aggregates.

- Natural gravels tend to be dense, so they have a surface, when ground, that's easier to seal than exposed lightweight aggregates, which are

porous. Also, lightweights are comparatively fragile and may chip when they're ground, leaving divots in the countertop. Thus we don't recommend lightweights unless the heavier weight of concrete made with natural gravel or crushed rock creates a problem that can't be solved through the design of the countertop or supporting structures.

- Natural gravel is more rounded than crushed rock, which has sharp, angular edges. Thus, natural gravel produces concrete that's easier to form and work than concrete made with crushed rock. (Some experts argue that crushed rock, because of its angles and sharp edges, has more surface area than natural gravel, mak-

▶ This natural river sand is typical of the sand you'll get from a batch plant. It's a graded sand with a mix of large to small particles. The sand shown here has formed clumps, indicating that it's moist, which is good (moist sand won't create lots of dust when you weigh and mix it).

▲ This lightweight aggregate, called expanded shale, is made from shale that has been crushed then heated in a kiln to high temperatures. Expanded shale is brown and tends to warm the tones of concrete. Because it's porous, expanded shale is hard to seal effectively after it has been exposed through grinding and polishing.

◄ A counter made from white cement and recycled glass by Counter Production. The glass was tumbled lightly and placed in the concrete mix, and the surface was ground and polished after setting.

BUYING AGGREGATE

When ordering readymix or when purchasing gravel for concrete you plan to mix yourself, ask for ⅜-in. pea gravel. This specifies gravel that has an MSA of ⅜ in. and a range of smaller sizes from ⅜ in. down to coarse sand. Be aware, though, that gravel tends to come from local sources, and depending on where you are, pea gravel may not be available. Also, pea gravel may not mean quite the same thing to all suppliers; by specifying pea gravel, you ought to get natural gravel, not crushed rock. If you have any doubts, find out exactly what you're going to get before you place an order.

Lightweight aggregates aren't as common as natural gravel, so you may have to take whatever is available when ordering readymix, or when purchasing lightweights for your own mix.

◄ Pea gravel is a natural aggregate typically found in alluvial fans. Because of its density, we like to use pea gravel when we plan to grind and polish the concrete.

ing possible more bonds with the cement paste and thus a stronger concrete, but this presumed advantage isn't significant enough to justify its use in an application such as a countertop.)

Admixtures

There are many admixtures available for concrete. Some of them speed setting time, some slow it down; some make concrete easier to pour, some are supposed to reduce cracking; some trap air, some prevent freezing; some prevent expansion while others promote it. We use only three admixtures in our mixes—a water reducer, polypropylene fibers, and (most of the time) pigments. If you're working in very hot conditions, you may want to consider a fourth admixture, a retarder.

Water reducer

A water reducer does just what the name suggests: It lets you use less water, while keeping the mix a workable consistency. And, remember, the less water you use, the stronger the concrete and the less risk of cracks.

There are dozens of water reducers on the market. We've had good results with Rheobuild 3000 FC from Master Builders Technologies. It includes a "plasticizer," a substance that helps concrete flow. The admixture produces a concrete with a very low water-to-cement ratio with normal workability. We usually use the maximum amount recommended by the manufacturer: 12 oz. per 100 lb. of cement.

This type of water reducer has a working life of about 60 min., at which

◀ Water reducer is an essential ingredient in concrete. It lets you produce a workable, plastic concrete mix with a minimum of water. The result is a strong concrete that's less likely to shrink and crack.

point the concrete begins to stiffen rapidly, so you'll need to have your pour very well organized so you can mix, place, vibrate, and finish off the back side of the piece within that period. If you order readymix (see the sidebar on p. 99), be aware that the concrete is hydrating during transit; if the trip from the plant to the site takes more than 30 min. or 40 min., plan on adding the water reducer or redosing once the concrete arrives, if it has begun to stiffen. If you plan to redose a batch of readymix, be sure to let your supplier know and read the instructions for the water reducer you plan to use; the instructions should tell you how much additional water reducer you can add per 100 lb. of cement. Be aware

that some water reducers are meant to be redosed; others cannot be.

Fibers

Fibers add strength to concrete, though it's not clear exactly how they work. One notion is that fibers strengthen concrete by preventing microcracks (very small cracks) from forming in the concrete. Another notion is that they don't prevent these cracks but rather keep them from growing. Some experts think that fibers also strengthen concrete by holding water in the cement paste, slowing water loss due to evaporation, and thus facilitating hydration and creating stronger bonds between the cement, aggregates, and rebar.

▶ Fibers can reduce the number of small cracks that tend to form in concrete; when cracks do form, the fibers keep them from growing.

There are many different fibers on the market, including glass, cotton, and steel fibers and several synthetics, including nylon and polypropylene fibers. We use polypropylene fibers almost exclusively, in particular a product called Stealth fibers (see Resources on p. 195). Polypropylene fibers are easy to work with, and they don't affect the surface texture or appearance of the finished concrete. No matter what kind you choose, all fibers need to be added carefully and slowly to concrete and mixed thoroughly or they'll tend to clump together.

Pigments

The most common and least expensive pigments are the blacks, the browns, and the reds—from carbon and mineral black and iron oxides. Blues and greens—from cobalt, ultramarine, and phthalocyanine blue; chromium oxide; and phthalocyanine green—are a bit more difficult to find, and they can be

USING FIBERS WITH A CAST-IN-PLACE COUNTER

If you're pouring a cast-in-place piece (see appendix 3), be aware that troweling pulls fibers up to the surface of the concrete, where they can be seen and felt, especially glass or steel fibers. The advantage of polypropylene fibers is that they're practically invisible and can be burned off with a torch if they're noticeable. Glass or steel fibers can't be burned off, though grinding will usually solve the problem.

If you're pouring in place and you're concerned about fibers rising to the surface, consider mixing two batches of concrete: one with fibers and one without. Pour the concrete with fibers into the bottom of the form, then a thin layer of concrete without fibers on top of that.

▲ A wide range of colors is possible with both powdered and liquid pigments. Most of these Syndecrete colors are combinations from a basic set of primary colors in white cement. Entirely different tones and hues are achieved by using gray cement.

much more expensive, depending on their source. We generally combine pigments ourselves to achieve the desired color, but you might want to try one of the many off-the-shelf, premixed colors from a variety of suppliers (see Resources on p. 195); these give reasonably predictable results.

When deciding on a color, be aware that lots of things can affect the finished look. For example, while all Type II and Type III cements are gray, different brands vary in shading, which can affect the color of the finished piece. Likewise, sand varies widely in color from locale to locale, and these variations can also affect the color. How you cure the piece, how (or whether) you grind it, and what you use to seal the concrete can also affect the color.

If an exact color is important, it's a good idea to make several samples (see the sidebar on p. 87) using a variety of color mixes and materials available in your area. Experiment to see how various ingredients, grinding, and sealing influence the finished look. Be aware that most concrete colors fade in sunlight, some more than others. Yellows and reds made with iron oxides are fairly stable in the sun. Blues and carbon black are more likely to fade to concrete's natural gray over time.

Pigments are measured as a percentage of the total weight of the cement being used. Because pigments tend to weaken concrete, as a rule of thumb, their total weight should not be more than 10 percent of the weight of the cement (the blue and black pigments

▼ Yellow iron oxide, ultramarine blue, red iron oxide, and chromium green are common pigments available from most concrete suppliers.

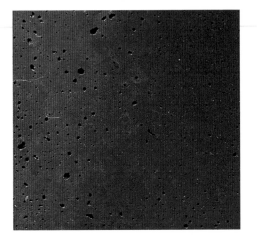

▲ This sample shows plum pigment in concrete made with gray cement. We measured the pigment to be 10 percent of the total weight of the cement. Pigments tend to weaken concrete, and 10 percent is about the maximum amount you ought to use.

▲ Grinding and polishing removes some of the most intensely colored cream, producing a surface with less color saturation.

▲ This sample of unground concrete was made with gray cement and ultramarine blue (8 percent) and carbon black (0.7 percent).

▲ When ground and polished, the blue-gray concrete loses some of its color intensity.

used in the piece featured here totaled 8.7 percent of the cement weight). We have, on occasion, pushed pigmentation to as much as 15 percent without problems, but at this level, there is a danger that the durability of the concrete's surface will be compromised. Generally, we try not to go overboard with pigments; intense colors look artificial, and we prefer the natural, earthy feel of more lightly colored concrete.

Retarders

If you're working in extremely hot conditions (temperatures above 90°F), you might consider using a retarder, especially if you're having readymix delivered over a long distance. A retarder is an admixture that keeps concrete plastic and workable for a longer period than it would be otherwise. We never use retarders because the weather in our part of the San Francisco Bay Area is

When ordering readymix, you may need to specify the amount of pigment by weight for the entire load, not just for the amount of concrete you plan to use. Since most ready-mix suppliers won't deliver less than a half a yard (and some may not deliver less than a full yard), this can be expensive if you're using lots of the higher-end blue or green pigments. If cost is a consideration, you might want to add the pigments to the readymix after it's delivered, assuming you have enough clean containers to hold it.

Also, not all readymix plants have a wide range of pigments (some may not have any pigments other than black). Thus you may need to get pigments from a local supplier or order them (see Resources on p. 195), then deliver the colors to the readymix plant to be included in your load. And be aware that some suppliers will tack on a surcharge for cleanup after delivering pigmented concrete.

rarely hot; also, retarders usually contain calcium, which may increase the risk of efflorescence (see p. 149).

If you're planning to have concrete delivered and the weather is likely to be hot, ask the contractor if he recommends a retarder and what kind. It might be a good idea to make some samples using some of the retarder to evaluate the admixture's effect on the finished surface.

A BASIC MIX

For our basic mix at Cheng Design, we use between six-and-a-half and seven 94-lb. bags of Type II or III cement per cubic yard of concrete; small aggregates; admixtures including water reducer and polypropylene fibers; varying amounts of pigment for color; and a minimum amount of water. All ingredients are measured by weight. The weights of the pigments are calculated in relation to the weight of cement. The water reducer we use calls for no less than 4 oz. or no more than 12 oz. per 100 lb. of cement; we typically use the maximum amount.

Calculated by cubic foot, our mix contains:

- Type II or Type III cement: 22.6 lb. for a 6.5-sack/cu.-yd. mix, or 24.3 lb. for a 7-sack mix (assuming 94-lb. sacks).

- ⅜-in. pea gravel: 37 lb. of natural aggregate or crushed rock with a

We measure all the ingredients in concrete by weight, even the water. Pigments and water reducer are calculated in proportion to the total weight of the cement. Amounts of fibers, cement, sand, and gravel are calculated by weight per volume of concrete.

maximum aggregate size of ⅜ in. (30 lb. of lightweight expanded shale).

■ Sand: 72 lb. of natural sand (40 lb. of lightweight sand).

■ Water reducer: 2.8 oz. of Rheobuild water reducer. The manufacturer specifies 4 oz. to 12 oz. for each 100 lb. of cement, and we always use the maximum recommended amount. Different brands will have different specifications, however, so be sure to read the directions.

■ Polypropylene fibers: About 0.6 oz. of fibers. The manufacturer of the fibers we use (Stealth fibers) specifies 1 lb. of fibers per cu. yd. of concrete. The amount you'll need will depend on the type of fiber.

■ Pigments: Amounts vary by weight as a percentage of the weight of the cement.

■ Water: Enough water, with water reducer, to create a mix that has the consistency of thick oatmeal. If you do a slump test (see the sidebar on

You can never have too many 5-gal. buckets when working with concrete. We use them for a variety of tasks, including measuring sand and gravel, storing measured ingredients, and carrying ingredients to the mixer.

p. 116), this would be enough water to create roughly a 2-in. slump before and a 4-in. slump after water reducer has been added.

Overall, this mix doesn't differ significantly from the mixes commonly used for sidewalks, driveways, foundations, or similar applications. Yet the small differences between these mixes can have a huge impact on the look and quality of the finished piece. The relatively high ratio of cement to sand and aggregates in our mix, the low water content, and the use of fibers produce a concrete that has high compressive strength and a minimum number of cracks due to shrinkage.

Compressive strength in itself isn't especially important in a piece like a countertop, which doesn't have to support much weight except its own, but concrete that has high compressive strength also has a hard, dense, durable surface, which is important. We've found that 6.5 sacks to 7 sacks of cement per cubic yard of concrete gives the best results; you can add more cement, which will create an even denser finish, but there's a law of diminishing returns at work here: The more cement you use in a concrete mix, the greater the risk the concrete will shrink and crack. (How the concrete is mixed, poured, and cured also affects compressive strength, the tendency to shrink, and the finished appearance, and we'll have more to say on this later in this chapter and in the chapters that follow.)

CALCULATING AND PROPORTIONING INGREDIENTS

Calculating how much of each ingredient you need and measuring each ingredient is a fairly straightforward process. All you need is a tape measure, a few clean 5-gal. buckets, a bathroom scale, and a calculator (or pen and notepad).

USING BAGGED CONCRETE

For projects of 9 cu. ft. or less, bagged concretes are a convenient alternative to the hassle of assembling and weighing out your own mix. In the past, the only bagged concretes available at local stores were the standard "5-sack" mix type, rated to 3,000 psi. The quality of these mixes can be uneven and it's hard to know how much cement is in them. If you are using this type of mix, add enough cement to create a mix that approximates a 6.5-sack mix.

Fortunately there are now high-quality bagged concretes available at most stores (Quikrete® 5000, for example). They cost a little more per bag, but the quality is worth it. They have a guaranteed rating to 5,000 psi and no additional cement is necessary. Adding the fibers, plasticiser, pigments, etc., makes a countertop-quality mix. A prepackaged kit of these additives is available. (See Resources on p. 195.)

We use readymix (mix delivered by truck from a batch plant) now and then, and we've had good results with it, but be aware that most plants won't deliver less than a half yard of concrete and some might deliver only a full yard. Even a half yard of concrete (13.5 cu. ft.) is two or three times as much as you'll likely need for a typical countertop. If you're going to order readymix, it's not a bad idea to have some other projects formed up and ready as well—a retaining wall, perhaps, or some stepping stones or a bit of walkway. Otherwise, you'll have a lot of waste to dispose of.

When ordering readymix, there are a number of things to keep in mind:

1. Call a week before to reserve delivery, then call the day before to confirm your order (some plants may need a longer lead time).

2. Specify how many sacks of cement you want (typically 6.5 sacks or 7 sacks) per yard of concrete.

3. Specify the type of aggregate and the maximum size aggregate (MSA)—for example, ⅜-in. pea gravel or ⅜-in. expanded shale. (Tell them you would like aggregates that are continuously graded from the fines up to the MSA.)

4. Specify the type and amount of fibers to be added at the plant.

5. Specify the type and amount of pigments, if you want them added at the batch plant (you may have to supply these yourself).

6. Give the people at the plant some directions regarding water content of the mix. Explain that you're pouring in a small area and that you want to control shrinkage, so you want the lowest water content possible. You might try specifying the "slump" (see p. 116), but not every batch plant is inclined to do such a test.

7. Specify the type and amount of water reducer to be added at the plant and find out how long the concrete will likely be in transit; you may need to redose at the site with more water reducer. Watch that the driver doesn't add water to the mix at the site. Because runny concrete flows more quickly, some drivers will try this approach so they can unload quickly and be on their way. If you're having the concrete pumped from the truck to the pour, the pumper may also be tempted to add water for the same reason.

8. Make sure you have plenty of clean wheelbarrows or other containers on-site, plus lots of help to handle the concrete once it arrives.

▲ When measuring the volume of the mold to calculate the amount of concrete you'll need, add 10 percent to the final figure.

BY THE WAY

If you're planning to pour samples at the same time you pour the main piece, don't forget to include the volume of the samples in your calculations.

Calculating ingredients

The first step is to determine the rough volume of your piece: Measure the length, width, and depth, taking the dimensions off the inside of the form. Measure the dimensions of any large knockouts, such as a sink knockout. Subtract the total for the large knockouts from the rough volume, then round up to the nearest foot. This will tell you how many cubic feet of concrete you'll need to fill your mold and any samples, with a little left over. (Because you'll want to end up with too much concrete rather than too little, it's not a bad idea to increase your final figure by 10 percent, to ensure a comfortable amount of extra concrete.)

To calculate the amount of dry ingredients needed:

1. Multiply the values given on p. 96 for 1 cu. ft. of cement, gravel, and sand by the number of cubic feet in your piece. For the countertop used as an example in this book, which contained 3 cu. ft. of concrete, we needed:

    ■ 22.6 lb. x 3 = 68 lb. of cement (for a 6.5-sack mix);

    ■ 37 lb. x 3 = 111 lb. of ⅜-in. pea gravel; and

    ■ 72 lb. x 3 = 216 lb. of sand.

2. Use the weight of cement (68 lb. in this case) to calculate the amount of water reducer. For our countertop, we used:

    ■ 8.2 oz. of water reducer for 68 lb. of cement (at 12 oz. per 100 lb. of cement).

3. Use the weight of the cement to calculate the pigments needed. To create the gray-blue color of our piece, we used:

    ■ 8 oz. of carbon black (0.7 percent of the weight of the cement in a 6.5-sack mix); and

    ■ 6 lb. of ultramarine (8 percent of the weight of the cement).

Measuring ingredients

We use a small kitchen scale for small amounts of pigment, fibers, and water reducer, and a portable, heavy-duty industrial scale for the cement and aggregates. However, a bathroom scale and some 5-gal. buckets will work just as well, even for very large amounts of sand and aggregate:

- Weigh a 5-gal. bucket on your scale, then put in only as much sand as you can lift comfortably.

- Weigh the bucket and sand, and subtract the weight of the bucket to get the exact weight of the sand.

- Level the sand and mark its height in the bucket with a black marking pen.

- Simply refill the bucket to the line to measure all of the sand you need. Do the same with the aggregates.

- Keep all the measured ingredients in several clean buckets or other containers, ready to add to the mix.

Managing water content

It takes about ¼ lb. of water by weight to thoroughly hydrate 1 lb. of cement;

▲ It doesn't take a lot of carbon black to darken concrete, which is already naturally gray. Other pigments vary in the effect they have on concrete's color. Reds are intense, for example, and you don't need much red pigment to give concrete a red cast. Blues aren't particularly intense, however; you'll need a high volume of blue in relation to the cement to significantly influence the color of the concrete.

▲ We use the maximum amount of water reducer recommended by the manufacturer. When having readymix delivered, we'll keep some additional water reducer handy to add to the mix if it begins to set up during transit.

▲ The manufacturer of these polypropylene fibers recommends 1 lb. per cu. yd. of concrete. Be careful not to handle the fibers in the wind.

▲ You can measure
sand and aggre-
gates on a
portable, heavy-
duty scale. In our
mix, we use 37 lb.
of pea gravel and
72 lb. of sand for
each cubic foot
of concrete.

this ratio of water to cement (0.25) produces the strongest concrete. However,
such a mix is too dry to work easily.
Thus the industry standard is a water-
to-cement ratio of 0.40, about 6.5 oz. of
water per pound of cement powder (not
mix) without water reducer.

Such specifications are okay for
rough work such as driveways or retaining walls, and they can be a good starting point for more exacting work
such as architectural pieces, but they
have limits.

The quantity of water you'll actually
need to properly hydrate a given mix
depends on a number of variables that
are likely to change from job to job and
even from day to day. For example,
more water is needed to hydrate concrete in hot, dry weather than on a
cold, damp day. Also more water is
necessary if the aggregates used happen
to be particularly porous. (It's a good
idea to presaturate porous lightweights
before adding them to the mix.) If the
aggregates are wet, however, or if the
sand is wet, you'll need to add much
less water to the mix than if the aggregates and sand have been sitting out in
a hot sun for several days. And to com-
plicate matters, sand and aggregates
that look merely "damp" can hold
deceptively large quantities of water;
it's easy to add too much water unless
you add it slowly and carefully in small
amounts, noting the effect on the mix
consistency.

Because water content is such an
important factor in the final appearance
of concrete, we almost never measure

◀ **Managing water content is something of an art. A mix that's too dry is hard to pour and vibrate; a mix that's too wet is likely to shrink excessively and crack. Properly hydrated concrete has the consistency of thick oatmeal. A ball of this concrete should roughly hold its shape when held in your hands.**

out all of the water in advance. Instead, we take a more roundabout approach, which ultimately gives us more control over the water content:

- First, we calculate by weight the amount of water we think we're likely to need. In this case, for 68 lb. of cement, that came to 27.6 lb. of water (at 6.5 oz. of water per lb. of cement).

- Next, we measure out half that amount of water (about 13.5 lb.).

- Then we add all of the water reducer we'll need for the entire batch of concrete to this measured water (in this case, 8.2 oz. of water reducer).

This mix of water and water reducer gives us a starting point. We add it slowly to the dry ingredients, while the mixer is running, then use a spray attachment on a hose to add additional water in small amounts until the mix has the consistency of thick oatmeal.

When holding a ball of properly hydrated concrete in your hands, it should roughly hold its shape; if you gently shake your hands, the concrete should flow into the recesses between your fingers. If it doesn't, it's too dry. If the concrete is soupy, though, it's too wet.

Of course, our "mixing by feel" approach may not be much help if you're mixing concrete for the first time or if you're accustomed to mixing concrete for slabs on grade. This is why we recommend doing a slump test periodically before you've added all of the water (see p. 116).

see p. 116

BY THE WAY

If your mold contains lots of rebar or complex shapes, tight angles, or several knockouts that are close together, you'll want a mix that is slightly wetter than thick oatmeal so the concrete can flow more easily.

CHAPTER 4

MIXING
AND POURING

oncrete can get unruly in a hurry, if your timing is off. Once you add water to aggregate, sand, and cement, there's no turning back; there won't be time to borrow or beg another cup of pea gravel or a bit more water reducer if you discover you've run out. When planning your pour, assume that once you add water, you'll have about 30 min. to 40 min. to mix, place, vibrate, screed, and trowel the concrete before it begins to set up.

To get the job done in such a limited time, you'll need to have all ingredients and all equipment where and when you need them. You'll also need enough people who know what they're doing; the lack of able hands at critical moments in a pour can scuttle an otherwise well-planned project. There

should be at least two of you, but three is better, especially if you're mixing several batches of concrete for a large piece.

French chefs have a name for such readiness: *mise en place*. It's the hallmark of a good professional kitchen, as it is of a good concrete pour.

TOOLS AND MATERIALS

At the most basic level, all you need to mix and pour concrete is a few bags of premixed concrete, some buckets or perhaps a wheelbarrow, a shovel or two, plenty of fresh water, and a finishing trowel.

Starting in this low-key way is a great way to introduce yourself to the process, have some fun, and (with a bit

▲ Calm after the storm: curing concrete after a pour.

BY THE WAY

If you haven't had much experience working with concrete, it's a good idea to use a slump cone (see the sidebar on p. 116) to measure the correct water content of your mix. You should be able to rent a slump cone where you rent your mixer.

of luck) end up with a useful piece of furniture. If you are working for the first time on a simple piece and you take this no-frills approach, it can give you confidence to try something more ambitious. You will be at the mercy of the quirks and idiosyncrasies of bagged premix concrete, however, so you'll need to be comfortable with surprises. Of course, concrete can be something of a revelation under even the most tightly controlled conditions. But that's part of the fun. The tools and materials described here will yield consistently good results time after time.

Mixing equipment

You can mix concrete in a wheelbarrow with a shovel, or even in a few 5-gal. buckets with a drill and mixing-blade attachment. But there's really no substitute for a good mixer; it's the best way to thoroughly combine all of your ingredients. Insufficiently mixed concrete will be hard to vibrate properly and can end up with dry spots, voids, areas of dull color, or hot spots (color that's too bright).

Be aware that portable mixers hold only about half the concrete indicated by their rated capacity; a rental with a rated capacity of 9 cu. ft. (typically the largest available) will hold only about 5 cu. ft. of concrete. Ideally, you'll mix all of your concrete in one batch, which could mean getting the largest portable mixer you can find (even a modest countertop of 6 ft. by 2 ft. by 3 in. contains 4 cu. ft. of concrete), or you might rent two smaller mixers. The other approach is to mix your concrete in several batches. This requires careful planning, however, such as making sure you have someplace clean to store one batch while you mix the next—a clean wheelbarrow perhaps or several 5-gal. buckets.

If you plan to color your concrete and intend to mix your pigment separately before adding the mix to the concrete, a ½-in. drill with a mixing blade will come in handy. So will a hose with a control nozzle and a source of clean water.

◀ ▲ Concrete can be mixed in just about anything: buckets, a wheelbarrow, or a washtub. The best way to thoroughly combine all the ingredients is to use a good mixer.

Equipment for moving and pouring concrete

Mixing concrete is a messy operation so we like to keep our mixers well away from the forms, and that means we have to have a way to move the concrete. For a small project requiring just a single batch of concrete, one wheelbarrow or a few buckets will do the job.

Vibrating the concrete

Concrete will need to be thoroughly vibrated once it's placed. Vibrating the concrete accomplishes a couple of important tasks: First, it causes the concrete to "liquefy" so that it flows into every crevice and around all the insets, knockouts, and rebar and remesh in the mold, and so that the fines in the mix flow around and between the larger aggregates, preventing the formation of voids. Second, vibrating the concrete helps remove any air that might be trapped in the mix; trapped air will form bubbles that create small holes and pits in the surface of the concrete as it sets up.

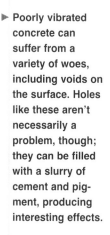
▶ Poorly vibrated concrete can suffer from a variety of woes, including voids on the surface. Holes like these aren't necessarily a problem, though; they can be filled with a slurry of cement and pigment, producing interesting effects.

▲ Vibrating concrete can be a low-tech endeavor. Here, the author (rear of the photo) and one of his crew work concrete into the tight spaces around knockouts by "massaging" the concrete with their fingers.

The safest method for vibrating a small piece like a countertop is to hold a palm sander, without sandpaper, tightly against the side of the form for a few moments, working around the perimeter. (A reciprocating saw, with the blade removed, will also work.) You'll get even more effective vibration with a sander if you wrap it in a couple of extra-strong plastic bags and place it on the wet concrete, taking care not to disturb the rebar and insets. This approach puts your sander in serious jeopardy, however; assume that if the bag tears, your sander will be ruined.

A low-tech method is to rap gently and rapidly on the sides of the form with a hammer. But the method that's by far the most fun is the lowest-tech method of all: Simply stick your gloved hands into the concrete and work it by hand into and around all the knockouts, inlays, and rebar, now and then wriggling your fingers quickly. If you can entice a friend or two to help, so much the better.

Sometimes, we'll use all three methods in the same pour, with good results.

There are a number of professional concrete vibrators available, and we'll

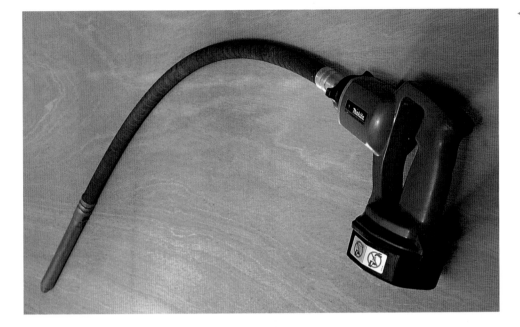

◀ **This cordless vibrator by Makita is perfect for small projects like countertops.**

often use them on larger pieces. Stick vibrators—"stingers"—come in a variety of sizes and configurations (most rental outlets that carry concrete supplies have stingers). Some stick vibrators are round, some are square. We like the square ones, and use the smallest available (¾ in. across).

Although stick vibrators are very effective, they have some serious drawbacks. For one thing, they're meant to be plunged into wet concrete; on a piece as shallow as a countertop, sticking the vibrator into the concrete raises the risk that you'll disturb the rebar and insets.

We suggest that if you use a stinger, run it along the surface of the wet concrete, taking care not to let it dip into the concrete so far that it disturbs the rebar, knockouts, or inlays. This technique is very effective. It's also very messy. (To cut down on the amount of concrete that will inevitably splatter on nearby walls, the floor, and you and

your colleagues, have a large piece of cardboard handy and someone to hold it over the vibrator as you move it along the concrete.)

Another option, which we don't recommend to anyone pouring concrete for the first time, is to clamp the stinger to the platform on which the form is built. This vibrates the entire work, keeps splatter to a minimum, and cuts the risk of mishaps with the insets and rebar. We do this on occasion, but we don't recommend it because a stinger can be dangerous if it comes loose. We've tried holding our stinger in place with C-clamps and bar clamps, but the vibrator inevitably works itself free, so we've come to rely on a heavy-duty bench vise.

Be aware that clamping the vibrator to the work has another risk: The vibration can shake apart the table to which it's clamped, and it can blow apart a poorly secured form. The table we use

▼ ► Clamping a stinger to the pour table is an effective way to vibrate concrete, but it's not a method that's recommended for beginners. Here, the stinger is held in a heavy-duty bench vise, and the table is reinforced to withstand the vibration.

is specially reinforced to take the abuse. There is also a type of vibrator (see Resources on p. 195) designed to be bolted to a table. This type is generally intended for use on a welded steel table, not a framework of 2x4s nailed together, and like the stinger, it can easily destroy a flimsy mold.

Finishing tools

You'll want a screed—a length of quality 2x4 or any other straight board will do—and a set of basic concrete fin- ishing tools, such as a wood float and a steel or magnesium trowel. You'll use these to smooth the bottom of the countertop as you would a sidewalk or other flatwork.

A set of basic concrete finishing tools. From left to right: magnesium and wood floats, a large steel finishing trowel, a rounded pool trowel (easier for beginners to use), and a small margin trowel.

Other equipment to have ready: plastic sheeting or perhaps a spray-on curing compound to control evaporation if the weather is hot and dry, or a space heater to warm the work during curing if the pour is done outdoors during cold weather (see chapter 5).

Safety equipment

Mixing and pouring concrete in small volumes is a relatively safe endeavor. However, there are a few potential hazards. You'll be using electrical equipment in wet conditions—always a risky situation—and you'll need the proper protection for your eyes, skin, and lungs.

- GFCI: Plug your mixer, vibrator, lights, heater, and any other power tools into ground-fault circuit interrupters (GFCIs). A GFCI is a circuit breaker that acts quickly to stop the flow of electricity in the event of a short circuit—for example, when you become part of the circuit. If permanent GFCIs aren't at the site, buy a portable GFCI or rig your own and plug all of your equipment into that, and then plug the GFCI into the permanent circuit.

- Safety glasses: Wear safety glasses while mixing and vibrating wet concrete and when grinding or polishing hardened concrete. The best safety

▶ Plan carefully where to set up your form and do the pour. Make sure you have enough room to work around the piece both during and after the pour.

fit over the ears; the second best are ear plugs.

■ Gloves: Use heavy-duty rubber gloves when handling and mixing the concrete, and surgical gloves (latex or nonlatex) when grinding, polishing, and sealing the cured concrete.

Tools for cleanup

You should have cleaned the form thoroughly before placing the insets and rebar, but it's a good idea to give the form another vacuuming just before pouring the concrete. Usually, one of us will be cleaning the form one last time while another is mixing the concrete.

If there's any concrete left over that we can't use, we let it harden, then dispose of it in a suitable waste facility. For the water used to clean the mixer and tools, we build a frame out of scrap 2x8s or 2x12s and plywood, which we line with plastic sheets. We place it by the mixer, so we can dump wash water into the temporary basin. We let the water evaporate, then dispose of the remaining solids along with the leftover concrete.

glasses are the wraparound style with polycarbonate lenses.

■ Face masks: When handling dry ingredients, wear a fitted charcoal-filter mask. A paper mask is better than nothing but offers minimal protection.

■ Hearing protection: Mixing wet concrete and grinding and polishing cured concrete are fairly noisy activities, so it's a good idea to protect your ears. The best hearing protectors

THE WORK ENVIRONMENT

Plan carefully where to set up your form and do the pour. The piece will have to remain in the form completely undisturbed for at least 3 days if you've used quick-cure Type III cement in the mix or about 5 days if you've used Type II cement.

You'll need ample room to work around the piece during the pour and then later as you peel away the forms, turn the piece, and finish the top. If the countertop is large, you may need to make provisions for turning the work with engine hoists (the kind with the heavy nylon straps, not chains) without damaging the still-fragile concrete, the structures around it, or yourself.

Finally, assume that you'll make a huge mess when you grind and polish the countertop after it has cured, so your workspace will have to be protected from water, grit, mud, and general gunk.

Consider your local climate as well. It's not a good idea to mix and pour concrete outdoors if the ambient temperature is above 90°F and the relative humidity is below 25 percent; besides the fact that it's no fun to work in such conditions, the concrete will set up too quickly, likely trapping air pockets and causing surface defects. If you can, wait until the evening to do the pour.

Nor is it a good idea to mix and pour when the temperature is below 50°F; in cold weather, the hydration reaction will slow nearly to a stop. And certainly you should never pour concrete in freezing weather. If you can, do the pour in a heated building in cold weather.

Also, if conditions during the 3 days to 5 days following the pour are likely to be very cold or very hot and dry, set up in a space that can be heated or kept moist, as needed, during the curing process. If you can't control the temperature and humidity in the workspace, have some way to heat the work or control evaporation around it (see chapter 5).

MIXING THE CONCRETE

The directions that follow assume that you have already calculated the volume of your piece (see chapter 3), plus enough extra concrete for any sample pieces, and that you've already measured out each ingredient: cement, aggregate, fines, fibers, pigment, water, and water reducer.

The dry ingredients

Add the aggregate to the mixer first, then the fines, and then let the mixer run for about 5 min., until these ingre-

BY THE WAY

If the sand and aggregates have been sitting out in the hot sun, sprinkle them with cool water just before putting them into the mixer. Also, use cold water to hydrate the mix, and shade or insulate the water lines. Concrete made with hot ingredients may set up too quickly.

◀ The aggregates and fines go into the mixer first, then the cement powder, a little at a time.

▶ Once the mix of water and water reducer has been added to the dry ingredients, add more water a little at a time. Concrete can go from too dry to too wet quickly, so keep an eye on the mix.

dients are thoroughly combined. Next, add the cement powder, a little at a time. Let the mixer run for a few more minutes. Keep the mixer as level as possible, without letting any of the contents spill out; the mixer will do a better job of mixing when it's level or nearly so.

Adding water

Remember that the amount of water you use is the single most critical factor in determining the final strength and finish quality of your concrete. As discussed in the previous chapter, we recommend mixing all of the water reducer into a small amount of water (in this case, 8.2 oz. of water reducer in roughly 13.5 lb. of water, about half the water we'll probably need to hydrate 68 lb. of cement).

With the mixer running, add the mix of water and water reducer to the dry ingredients a small amount at a time. Don't just pour the water into the mixer; rather, distribute it as evenly as possible over all of the dry ingredients. Otherwise, some areas of the mix can soak up a lot of water, leaving other areas less well hydrated.

Once you've added all of the mixture of water and water reducer, let the mixer run a moment, then use a hose with a spray nozzle to add more water. Concrete tends to go from too thick to too runny in a hurry, so add the water slowly, keeping an eye on the consistency of the mix as you do so.

Be especially cautious if the sand and aggregates are already wet; they can hold a deceptive amount of water, and it's easy to add too much water to already saturated materials.

◄ The less water in the mix, the stronger the finished concrete. Concrete like this, with the consistency of thick oatmeal, is about right for a countertop: it's stiff, but wet enough to be workable.

As noted previously, we've learned from experience what concrete looks like when it contains the proper amount of water—the least water needed to thoroughly hydrate the cement and make a workable mix that will cure without shrinking or cracking. The mix should look like thick oatmeal.

But advice about "eyeballing" the mixture to determine the correct hydration isn't going to be much help if you haven't had much experience with concrete—or with oatmeal. That's why we recommend doing a slump test (see the sidebar on p. 116). After mixing a few batches, you'll develop a feel for the correct water content and you can dispense with the test.

If you find that you've added too much water to the mix and are mixing only one batch, perhaps the simplest

and safest approach is to dump the concrete and start over, assuming you have enough additional ingredients. If you're mixing several batches, set the wet one aside, then mix the others and place them first. By the time you get to the wet batch, it might have stiffened a bit. Put this one into the mold last.

Another option would be to add a little more cement powder, aggregate, and sand to the mix, roughly in the proportions used for the entire batch: 0.6 to 1 to 2, respectively. Start with small amounts, noting their effect on the concrete's consistency. This approach can be tricky; it's very easy to add too much of a dry ingredient.

BY THE WAY

If you're mixing several batches, keep some water reducer in reserve; you may need to add more to the first batch if it begins to stiffen while you mix the others. Be sure to follow the manufacturer's recommendations for "redosing" concrete.

The best way to determine the correct hydration of a batch of concrete is to perform a slump test. For this test, you'll need a slump cone. To use the cone:

1. Moisten the inside of the cone and put it on a smooth, level surface such as a moist piece of plywood or a concrete slab.

2. Fill the cone one-third full with a sample of concrete. The directions in the definitive Concrete Manual recommend tamping this con-crete exactly 25 times with a tamping rod measuring ⅝ in. dia. and 24 in. long. The manual specifically states that you shouldn't use a piece of rebar. Of course, the manual is for those involved in big commercial operations. If rebar is all you have, relax and use it. (By "tamping," the manual means running the rod up and down in the concrete so it completely fills the cone and is free of air pockets.)

3. Fill the cone with a second layer until it's two-thirds full, and tamp this layer so the tamping rod penetrates but doesn't go through the first layer.

4. Add more concrete until the cone is slightly over-filled and tamp this layer.

5. Scrape off the excess concrete.

6. Slowly lift the cone away from the concrete.

7. Put the cone beside the concrete but not touching it. Rest a straightedge across the cone and measure the distance down to the top of the sample.

A good mix for finished architectural concrete should have a slump of 4 in. with water reducer added. If you're working in very hot, dry conditions or if the mold has lots of intricate shapes around which the concrete must flow smoothly, you may want a slightly wetter mix, keeping in mind that the more water in the mix, the higher the risk of cracks.

▲ The slump cone is a 12-in.-high sheet-metal cone, with an 8-in.-dia. base and a top that's 4 in. in diameter.

▲ This concrete is a bit too stiff. It will be difficult to pour and vibrate properly, raising the risk of voids.

▲ This concrete has about a 4-in. slump. It's wet enough to be poured and vibrated properly yet dry enough that, as it cures, it will reach maximum strength.

▲ Excessive slump means the concrete has too much water. It's likely to shrink excessively and crack. It will be significantly weaker than properly hydrated concrete.

For uniform color saturation in the concrete, mix the pigments in a little water, then add to the other ingredients. For varied color saturation, add dry pigment a little at a time.

Adding pigments and fibers

There are two ways to add pigment. Perhaps the simplest is to add the powder to the mix a little at a time. Don't dump all of the pigment in at once or some of it is likely to billow out of the mixer, perhaps enough to affect the color of the finished piece.

Sometimes we mix all of the pigment into a small amount of the water first, then add this pigmented water to the dry ingredients, followed by the mix of water and water reducer, and finally enough additional clear water to give us the desired hydration. When mixing more than one batch of concrete,

add equal amounts of pigment or pigmented water to each batch.

Add the polypropylene fibers a little at a time after you've added some of the water. If you add fibers to dry ingredients or add them in large amounts, a significant amount of the fibers will likely billow out of the mixer.

Once you've added all the ingredients, let the mixer run for 7 min. Shut it off and let the mix "rest" for 10 min. During this time, the materials in the mix will continue to absorb the water you've added, and the mix will likely stiffen a bit. Turn the mixer on and spray in a little more water to bring the

BY THE WAY

Be sure to wear a mask, gloves, and goggles when handling pigments. Also, be aware that if you get any pigments on your clothing, especially blues and reds, you'll never get the stains out.

These Chinese coins float in a sea of blue concrete. By adding pigments separately while placing the concrete in the mold, the intensity and location of the color can be controlled.

BY THE WAY

You can place the first batch of concrete in the form before mixing the next, but we don't recommend it. Once you've placed any concrete in the form, you're committed. If something goes wrong with the next batch—if you realize you've miscalculated the amount of cement you'll need and you've run out, or if your mixer suddenly dies—it's difficult to clean out the concrete you've already placed, and your form may be ruined. It's simpler and less costly to mix a new batch of concrete than it is to make a new form.

mix back to the correct viscosity, then mix for another 7 min.

Once all ingredients are thoroughly mixed, there are two things you can do with this batch. If this is the only batch you will make, move on to the next step (see "Placing the Concrete" on the facing page). If you're going to be mixing more batches, pour this first batch into a clean wheelbarrow or another clean container and set the concrete aside. Next, rinse the mixer and let it drip dry for a moment—the clock is ticking—then add a small amount of the dry ingredients, let them turn in the mixer for a moment to absorb some of

the excess water, stop the mixer and break up any clumps that form, then add the rest of the ingredients, as instructed previously.

While one person is mixing the second batch, another should keep an eye on the first batch—especially if the weather is hot and dry—stirring it occasionally if the concrete looks like it's beginning to tighten up. If the first batch begins to stiffen, add more water reducer according to the manufacturer's recommendations for redosing.

▲ Polypropylene fibers add strength to the concrete by keeping cracks to a minimum. Add them carefully, in small batches.

▲ A single color, added to a concrete mix unevenly, can produce compelling results.

PLACING THE CONCRETE

Once all the concrete is mixed, take the first batch you mixed and gently distribute the concrete evenly throughout the bottom of the form. Don't push this first layer of concrete around on the form; this may dislodge the insets or even scratch the form.

Vibrate this first layer until it flows completely and evenly over the bottom of the form. If you're vibrating the entire table with a stinger or the type of vibrator that bolts onto the table, bubbles should appear on the surface of the concrete as air is vibrated out of the mix. Keep vibrating until fewer new bubbles are formed. This should take

only a moment. Insufficient vibration will lead to voids—unfilled spaces between the aggregates or small holes on the surface caused by air trapped in the concrete (see chapter 5 for fixes). It is possible to overvibrate concrete using a vibrating table or a stinger plunged into the concrete. When you over-vibrate, the larger aggregates can sink to the bottom of the wet concrete. This can affect the surface appearance and weaken the concrete.

If you're pouring in several batches, we don't recommend running a vibrator across the surface of the first layer of concrete; it's too easy to disturb the rebar and inlays when there isn't a thick layer of concrete above them.

BY THE WAY

Before vibrating the concrete, make sure that none of your wire ties holding the rebar and remesh cage in place have come loose. If the cage isn't held firmly in place, it will sink like a rock once the vibrator is turned on.

PLACING THE CONCRETE

▼ ▶ Two pairs of hands are better than one. Concrete can begin to stiffen quickly, so while one person places the concrete, the other can work it into tight places, making sure there are no voids that will weaken the piece.

It's almost impossible to overvibrate the concrete using a palm sander or by agitating the concrete with your gloved hands or simply rapping on the form with a hammer. But it is quite possible to undervibrate it, so take your time to vibrate the concrete thoroughly.

Once the first batch has been placed and vibrated, place more of the concrete, vibrating each batch. Toward the end, you may need to pour small amounts of concrete to fill in low areas, typically around the faucet and sink knockouts. Be careful not to overfill the mold; the concrete will be easiest to screed if just enough concrete is placed in the mold so that a small amount is pushed ahead of the screed as it's passed across the form.

Screed the concrete using a clean, straight 2x4 or other straight piece of wood. Work the board across the surface of the concrete in a sawing motion. As you screed and then trowel the concrete, you can top off the concrete a little at a time, if needed.

After screeding, wait until the concrete has dulled—about 20 min. to 30 min.—then use a wooden float to further smooth the concrete, making sure all the aggregate is just below the surface. If water appears on the surface as you float it, stop and wait until the water disappears and the surface becomes dull again.

After floating the concrete, give it a chance to set up before troweling.

▶ It's most effective to vibrate concrete in layers, rather than all at once. Once the first layer has been vibrated, add more and vibrate the concrete again.

◀ Here, the concrete has just been placed but hasn't been vibrated. It's thick and already beginning to set up.

◀ During vibration, the gelatinous concrete quickly liquifies and settles, flowing around the rebar and remesh, the knockouts, and any inlays. Air trapped in the concrete should rise to the surface, forming bubbles.

◀ Vibration is complete when only a few bubbles rise to the surface. This should take only a moment. Properly vibrated concrete will be free of blowholes and voids and will cure to maximum strength.

Leave the wire rebar hangers in place and work the screed over them until you're absolutely certain you don't intend to vibrate the concrete again. When you're ready to cut the wires, cut them below the surface of the concrete, then smooth the concrete with a trowel.

▲ A board with a clean, straight edge makes an effective screed. Use a sawing motion to work the screed forward. A little concrete should mound up ahead of it.

▶ Use a shorter screed for small areas.

This may take anywhere from 25 min. to 90 min., depending on the weather. The concrete is ready to be troweled if it gives only slightly when you press your finger against it. Use the steel trowel, holding it nearly flat against the con-crete for the first pass; if it's not held flat enough, you risk creating a rough, "washboard" surface. Troweling should bring up a sheen on the surface of the concrete but no water. If water appears, back off and wait. After this troweling,

▲ Concrete at rest, between screeding and the first floating.

◀ Check to make sure the mold is completely filled after vibrating and screeding; any dips along the edge of the mold may show once the countertop is installed.

wait a few minutes to let the concrete set a bit more, then trowel it again, this time holding the trowel at a slight angle, as you would when troweling a sidewalk or other flatwork.

Carefully check the level of the concrete along the edges of the form, particularly any edges that will be visible once the piece is in place. Make sure that the concrete is completely and evenly filled along the edge of the form. Even small voids or irregularities along the edge will show.

Move immediately on to curing (see chapter 5).

CHAPTER 5

CURING, FINISHING, AND TROUBLE-SHOOTING

"All materials derive from nature. By subtly revealing the source—grinding the surface of concrete to reveal aggregate and embedded semiprecious stones, for example—we create understated references to nature while celebrating the hand of man."

—Fu-Tung Cheng

In the previous chapter, you learned how to control the many variables in mixing and pouring concrete that can affect the material's appearance and long-term durability. How the concrete is cured can also influence the quality and look of the finished piece, and in this chapter we'll describe how to control this process. We'll discuss various finishing techniques and how these can alter or enhance concrete's appearance. Finally, we'll look at the various ways you can fix those less-than-pleasant surprises that sometimes result from even the most meticulous pour.

CURING

Curing refers to the process of controlling the temperature and the moisture content of new concrete to promote hydration. The ideal conditions for curing concrete are high humidity (to slow water loss) and a concrete temperature between 70°F and 75°F (a range of 55°F to 85°F is acceptable) during the first 3 days to 7 days after the concrete has been mixed and poured. This is the period when the hydration reaction is progressing most rapidly and fresh concrete is most susceptible to environmental extremes. Temperature and humidity become less important after that.

Concrete that's cured under unfavorable conditions can end up cracked and weakened, with a host of surface blemishes such as efflorescence (mineral deposits on the surface) and water stains.

▲ No one really knows why one piece will effloresce and another won't. It can be an ingredient, conditions during curing, or any number of other imponderables. Fortunately, it's easily fixed by leaching with water or by grinding.

when the temperature rises and the humidity drops.

In most parts of the country, the environment is likely to be a bit more unruly—too hot, too cold, too dry—so unless you live in the Bay Area, you may need to heat, cool, or wet the concrete to ensure it cures properly.

If you're experienced working with concrete slabs on grade, some of the procedures outlined below will be familiar. However, some standard practices that are entirely appropriate for common slab work or foundations can be inappropriate for precast, or cast-in-mold, concrete. We'll note where special precautions are needed.

Controlling temperature

Curing concrete in hot, humid weather won't present significant problems, as long as the concrete is kept moist, below 100°F, and out of direct sun and wind. But cold temperatures will cause trouble. Hydration slows significantly at temperatures below 55°F, and the temperature of curing concrete should never be allowed to fall below freezing during at least the first 7 days after being poured. If the water in fresh concrete freezes, the bonds between the aggregate and cement will break, and the concrete will never become as strong or as durable as it should be.

Obviously, if you're curing the piece in a heated room, you don't need to worry about the temperature; just keep the thermostat set between 70°F and 75°F (ideally, the temperature of the concrete shouldn't be allowed to drop below 55°F while it cures). If you're

Of course, in some environments, proper curing will take place without much intervention. In the San Francisco Bay Area, for example, where we have our shop and where we make our countertops, the weather is fairly moderate year-round: Winter weather tends to be cool and damp, with daytime temperatures in the 50s and 60s and nighttime lows that rarely get even close to freezing. Summer weather tends to be mild, moderated by the fog bank that forms over the cold Pacific waters and invariably drifts inland each evening and retreats each morning.

It's an almost ideal climate for working with concrete. Even so, we aim for consistent curing conditions, so we generally warm our pieces for at least the first 72 hr. after pouring—summer and winter—and we sometimes take steps to control moisture loss on those rare days

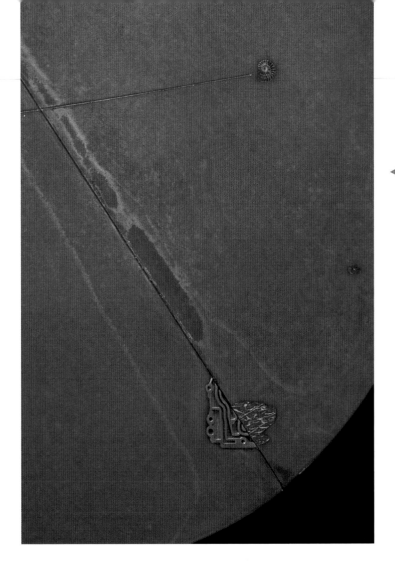

◀ Integral mineral colors, a transmission part, and inlaid amazonite stone animate a purple-hued countertop.

working in an unheated shed or garage, then you'll need to directly heat the piece. Tent the piece with plastic sheeting and heat it with an electric space heater or, if your local equipment rental outlet has one, a portable steam generator. Try to keep the temperature in the tent between 70°F and 75°F.

Controlling moisture loss

The worst enemy of fresh concrete is a hot, dry, windy day. If surface water is allowed to evaporate from the exposed side of freshly poured concrete, water in the interior of the piece will wick out, causing excessive shrinkage and cracking. Water loss can also affect the color of pigmented concrete, typically resulting in duller tones than intended. In the worst case, if too much water evap-

orates from the concrete, the hydration reaction will simply stop—remember, hydration is a chemical reaction that needs sufficient water to take place. If hydration stops, the concrete will never reach full strength.

The usual approach to protecting freshly poured concrete slabs and sidewalks in hot, dry conditions is to keep sprinklers misting the surface or to cover the concrete with wet burlap sacks, old rugs, or towels, and perhaps plastic sheeting on top of that. Many professionals spray a water-based curing compound on the slab to slow water loss.

These practices work well on concrete slabs and foundations, but with the exception of the curing compounds, they can cause problems with cast-in-mold concrete: Water from wet cover-

BY THE WAY

Fresh precast concrete should not be moved or disturbed in any way. Curing begins immediately after pouring, so try to anticipate and plan for any weather changes that could take place during the first week or so after you've poured the piece—sudden heat waves, cold snaps, dry winds, etc.—and be prepared to protect the green concrete, wherever it is, from all possible extremes.

▶ **Water from wet coverings can leak into the mold and pool under the concrete, leaving water stains and other blemishes.**

necessary; there are simpler methods that work as well.

We prefer not to cover our pieces as they cure because this helps facilitate water migration away from the bottom of the mold (and thus away from what will be the finished surface of the piece). We've found that not covering our pieces helps prevent water stains and other blemishes. A little water probably does evaporate but, under most conditions, too slowly to cause problems. If we need to slow or prevent moisture loss, we'll cut a sheet of plastic about 1 in. smaller all around than the piece, and lay it directly on the concrete; this slows water loss without the problem of water running down inside the mold. Rarely, in the very hottest, driest conditions, we'll cover the entire countertop in a tent of plastic sheeting. We spread the plastic over a wooden framework, taking special care not to let the tent touch the concrete or the mold. This keeps any water that condenses on the plastic sheeting from running down into the mold and under the concrete.

Curing time

How long do you need to control the temperature and humidity around curing concrete? The answer depends on the weather conditions and on whether or not you plan to polish or grind the piece.

As a rule of thumb, concrete made with Type III ("high-early") cement should cure for no less than 3 full days (72 hr.). Concrete made with Type II cement should be cured for 5 days or longer. In a cool, unheated environ-

BY THE WAY

Professional precasters and concrete-countertop manufacturers often set up curing rooms that use steam heat to accelerate the turnaround cure time to 24–48 hr.

ings will leak into the mold and pool under the concrete, leaving water stains and a variety of other blemishes. Usually, these stains and blemishes can be polished out. But fewer stains, of course, mean less polishing. We have on occasion used the water-based curing compounds, but given our damp, mild climate, we've found that they aren't ment, however, it's not a bad idea to leave any concrete in the mold, controlling for moisture loss, for 2 weeks to 3 weeks, if possible.

If you intend to grind the concrete to expose sand or aggregate (see "Grinding" on p. 139), it's best to break the piece out of the mold sooner rather than later: after 72 hr. if Type III cement was used or 5 days for Type II cement. The concrete is durable at this point but not yet rock hard, so grinding will be a lot easier on you, your equipment, and your pocketbook—the diamond grinding pads are expensive, from $35 to $70 per pad, depending on the fineness of

the grit. Be aware, however, that concrete this green is easily gouged by any bits of grit or aggregate that break loose during grinding, so you'll need to work slowly and with care.

Wait for about 10 days before polishing the concrete with the finest pads; freshly cured, still-green concrete is too soft to be polished effectively.

▼ A concrete countertop by Paco Prieto was cast around this granite sink from China. It was poured from the top with aggregate, with the sink in place. After curing, the sink was removed and the surface ground.

RELEASING THE CONCRETE

The moment when the piece is ready to be removed from the mold is always a moment of great anticipation—and some trepidation. A cast-in-mold piece is most vulnerable when the mold is being removed. The concrete is still green at this point and easily damaged, so great care will be required.

You won't need many tools to release the form—just a hammer, a prybar, a nail puller, a screwdriver, Vise-Grips, a few clean wooden shims, and some patience.

▶ You'll need a few basic tools to get the countertop out of the mold.

Examining the piece

The first step is to carefully check the edges of the concrete around the mold, especially along any edges that will be exposed to view once the piece is in place. Look for areas that may not have been completely filled to the top of the mold during the pour: Any such dips in the concrete will likely be noticeable when the piece is installed. Of course, you already looked for and filled any low spots while screeding and finishing the wet concrete, but if you missed any, this final check provides the opportunity for an easy fix.

Fill any low spots along an exposed edge with a mixture of PC7 or PC11 epoxy resin (see Resources on p. 195), with pigment added to approximate the color of the concrete. PC7 epoxy is gray, for use with concrete made with gray cement, and PC11 is white, for use with concrete containing white cement. These epoxies bond to hardened concrete more securely than does a cement/sand mix, which makes them ideal for fixing chipped or uneven edges. They also keep their color when they harden, making it fairly easy to match the color of the concrete. These epoxies stiffen in 1 hr. to 3 hr., and they're quite hard in 24 hr. to 48 hr. Use a broad putty knife to work the epoxy and pigment paste into the low spots, taking care that the fill is even with the top of the mold. Let the epoxy fill harden completely before removing the sides of the mold.

Removing the mold

Start by unfastening all screws used to hold the mold to the table and the backer boards to the mold. If you counted the screws as you put them in, make sure you've removed the same number. Remember: If you leave in a screw, especially one holding the mold to the table, there's a danger of twisting and cracking the piece when you try to move it.

To remove the sides of the mold, gently work the prybar between the end of a side piece and the end piece at one corner, being careful to keep the prybar away from the concrete. Use the prybar to pry one end of the side piece far enough away from the concrete so that you can work your fingers into the gap. Gently pull back, taking care not to pull so hard that the side piece breaks (a mold, or pieces of it, can be reused). A slight tension on one end should be enough to spring the melamine. Do the same with the other side piece. For the two ends, tap on the top edge of the melamine with the prybar, taking care not to touch the concrete. This should be enough to pop the piece loose. If it doesn't, gently work a clean wooden shim into the hairline gap between the concrete and the mold wall. Tap gently on the shim until the piece comes free. If the knockout still won't come loose, work a flat prybar between the shim and the melamine and pry it free.

Remove the backer boards from the sink knockout. Then, tapping gently on a prybar placed against the MDF, free the sides of the sink knockout from the concrete. The melamine should peel off easily. If it doesn't, shoot a screw into

◀ **Make sure you remove all the screws holding the mold to the table. If you miss one, you risk twisting the mold and cracking the concrete when you try to move it.**

▲ **The side pieces usually pop off without a lot of coaxing. Pry them away from concrete enough to work your fingers under, then pull gently.**

▲ **Always lever against the mold, not the concrete.**

► The backer boards and sides for the sink knockout should be pried out carefully; the still-green concrete is easily marred.

► The sink void, with knockouts removed.

BY THE WAY

If your piece has a divide (like the countertop featured here)—with the mold bottom as one piece—remember that the countertop itself is in fact two (or more) separate pieces. You'll need enough people on hand to support and safely turn both pieces at one time. Talk every move out in advance, so that everyone involved knows what to do and when.

the side of the knockout and pull on the screw with some Vise-Grips.

Next, remove the faucet and air-gap knockouts. Back off the single long screw that holds each knockout in place, enough to free it from the bottom of the mold. Then use a nail puller to pull out the screw and the plug. (It's all right to pry against the concrete because this is the bottom of the piece and won't show and it's not near an edge.) Later, once the bottom of the mold has been removed, you can use a small piece of wood to knock the PVC out of the hole.

Use a diamond sanding pad (about 400 grit) to slightly ease the corners of the sink knockout and all around the edges of the countertop, as shown in the bottom photo on p. 134. Concrete

 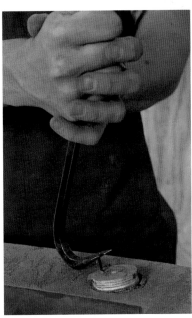 

◄ To remove faucet or air-gap knockouts, drive a drywall screw into the edge of the knockout, then pry up with a prybar or pull out with Vise-Grips. It's all right to pry against what will be the bottom of the countertop, but don't get too close to the fragile edge.

right out of the mold has edges that are sharp enough to cut unprotected fingers; blunting the edges makes the countertop a little more comfortable and safer to handle. Eased edges are also less likely to chip.

To remove the bottom, you'll need to turn the piece over. First, slide it to the edge of the table so that almost half of it hangs over the edge. Carefully tilt the countertop so you can work several pieces of 1-in. rigid foam insulation under the other edge.

Tilt the countertop up on one edge (make sure you have lots of help for this part), taking care not to flex the piece (twisting the green concrete even slightly can crack it). Place additional pieces of rigid foam on the table, and carefully lower the countertop onto them. Again, be very careful not to flex the countertop, and remember that, at this point, there's nothing but suction holding the mold bottom to the

countertop, so be sure to hold on to both firmly.

To remove the mold bottom, first try pulling up on one corner by hand. Often the mold bottom will just pop free with very little coaxing. If it won't come loose easily, work a clean wooden shim between the concrete and the mold bottom and tap on it lightly; this might loosen the bottom. If not, try working a flat prybar between the shim and bottom and gently pry up, as shown in the photo at left on p. 136. If necessary, work more shims along the edge of the mold bottom until it pops free.

Use these same techniques to remove a knockout for an integral drainboard, like the one on this countertop. This particular knockout turned out to be more difficult to remove than the rest of the form; the Plexiglas strips were slightly chipped, allowing concrete to seep under them and harden. This

BY THE WAY

Before you lower the countertop, be careful to place the foam so that the narrow arms around the sink knockout are supported at the bases, not at their ends. Supporting the arms at their ends can cause cracking.

1. Slide the countertop to the edge of the table so that it's hanging over the edge, and put a few pieces of rigid foam insulation under the inside edge.

2. Turning a large concrete piece is a delicate process. Have plenty of help on hand, and rehearse the steps before beginning.

3. Because suction is the only thing holding the concrete to the bottom of the mold, everyone should keep a firm grip on the countertop and the mold.

◀ Concrete fresh out of the mold will have sharp edges. To prevent chipping and to protect your hands, ease the edges while the concrete is still green and soft.

locked the strips into the concrete, and when we pulled the knockout up, small bits of concrete chipped out along with the Plexiglas. (To find out how we fixed this, see "Troubleshooting" on p. 149).

Once the mold bottom has been removed, knock the PVC out of the faucet and other similar knockouts with a block of wood.

4. Put more foam insulation down, then carefully lower the countertop onto it, taking care not to flex the piece.

5. With the turn complete, slide the countertop back to the center of the table.

◀ ▼ Gently lift one corner of the mold bottom to get a feel for how stubborn it will be. Often, it will simply pop loose.

▲ Stubborn pieces of the mold bottom, such as this drainboard knockout, can be loosened by carefully tapping a few wooden shims along one edge. If that doesn't work, use a prybar to gently lever against a wooden wedge.

▲ Slide the edge of the countertop off the table, and use a small block of wood to drive out the PVC sleeve in the faucet and air-gap knockouts.

Cleanup

Any inlays embedded in the concrete's surface will probably be covered with some of the silicone caulk used to secure them to the mold, as well as a bit of flashing—fine, dried cement—which usually seeps under them and hardens. Use a razor to scrape away the caulk and flashing.

GRINDING AND POLISHING

We recommend grinding and polishing the countertop to expose some of the fines and aggregate. This creates a surface that is visually interesting. Such a surface is also practical because the complex colorings and patterns of exposed fines and aggregate don't show stains as easily as a more uniform visual

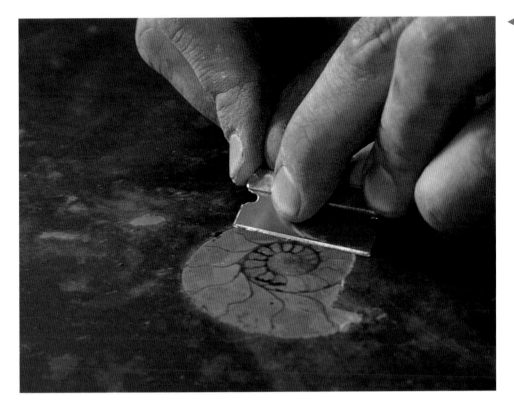

plane. Grinding and polishing also allow any patches or fills in voids to be seamlessly disguised, and the process removes common blemishes such as water stains, discolorations where water might have leached out of the mold, and uneven surfaces.

Grinding and polishing are not nearly as laborious or as exacting as they once were: Tools and pads have improved vastly in the past 10 years. If you begin the finishing process before the concrete has become hard—within the first 10 days after pouring (if your concrete was made according to the recipe in this book, it gets hard quickly)—grinding is a relatively easy task.

To grind and polish the concrete, you'll need the following:

■ **A variable-speed grinder/ polisher.** These are available from tool-rental outlets. We use a Fein grinder, which has speeds from 900 rpm to 2,700 rpm and an electronic feedback system that keeps the speed constant at any pressure. It also has a ⅝-in. arbor, which accepts a Velcro-based disk for matching Velcro-backed diamond pads. We like the Velcro binding system because it allows us to change pads quickly. The system also allows us to put each pad on the disk slightly off center, which creates a random grinding pattern and reduces the risk of deep scratches or noticeable cut marks in the concrete.

▲ The countertop, free of the mold. Note the water stains and the chips around the slots for the brass rails; both problems are easily fixed.

▲ The concrete has perfectly reproduced the texture of the melamine mold. Grinding and polishing will smooth the surface.

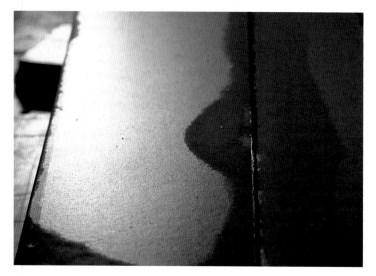

▲ This water stain, caused by water that pooled under the concrete, will disappear with light grinding.

▲ Inlays that pop out, like one of the three Chinese coins that came loose when the mold was removed, can be glued back in with PC7 epoxy.

- **A set of diamond grinding pads.** We typically use 3M pads, in grit sizes of 60, 120, 220, 400, 600, 800, and 1,200. They range in price from $35 for the finest to more than $70 for the coarsest. Finer pads than 1,200 grit are available, but we rarely use them (more on this later). We also use hand pads of the same grit sizes to get into tight places.
- **A water supply and a large squeegee.**
- **A GFCI**, because you'll be using an electrical device around water. (We also recommend heavy-duty rubber gloves and rubber boots as additional protection against electric shock.)

- **Appropriate safety gear including goggles and ear plugs.**

Grinding

Before you begin, clean the countertop thoroughly. Run water over the surface, then squeegee it off to remove any grit that might have settled on the piece. Any grit left on the surface can gouge the green concrete if you grind over it.

Start grinding with the coarsest pad appropriate to the finish you're trying to achieve. If you want to expose a broad range of rocks and sand, start with the 60-grit pad. This pad and the next finer pad (120 grit) will give you the basic "look" in terms of exposed

BY THE WAY

If you've never ground or polished concrete before, make sure to practice on some samples before attacking your finished piece.

▲ This cast-iron grate was troweled into the concrete and ground. The size of the aggregate is a consequence of aggressive grinding.

▲ To grind and polish concrete, use a variable-speed grinder and a set of diamond pads—from 60 grit to 1,200 grit.

aggregate. If you don't want to expose lots of aggregate, start with the 120-grit pad or perhaps even the 220 grit. If you start with the 60-grit pad, be aware that this pad will create a very rough surface, and to smooth it completely, you'll need to work progressively through all the pads to the finest—no small task. If you try to take a shortcut by jumping from a very coarse pad to a much finer pad, you'll find it's difficult to smooth the concrete effectively.

Make sure you have a constant water supply to keep the piece wet as you grind; if you dry-grind or fail to provide enough water to clear the (very expensive) pads, you'll quickly wear them out. The Fein grinder has an attached, adjust-able water feed that puts out a steady stream of water ahead of the grinder. If your grinder doesn't have such a feed, a friend with a hose will do. If you're working alone, fill a plastic bottle with water, poke a few small holes around the bottom, and put it on the counter-top near the area you're grinding.

As you grind with the coarsest pads, periodically stop and squeegee the entire surface to check that you've exposed as much aggregate as planned and that you've done so evenly. Cleaning the surface regularly will also remove any small bits of debris that might gouge the still-green concrete.

Once the fines and aggregates appear evenly and consistently exposed over

▶ Hold the grinder as flat as possible and apply even pressure. Be sure to keep the concrete thoroughly wet as you grind. If your grinder doesn't have a built-in water supply, a plastic bottle with a few nail holes in the bottom will work well.

the entire surface, put on the 120-grit pad and go over the surface again, stopping to squeegee off the water now and then to check that you're covering the surface evenly.

It's all right to grind over inlays such as fossils, but lighten up a bit when using the coarsest pads. Be sure to grind all exposed edges as well as the top surface.

Repeat the process with the 220-, 400-, and 600-grit pads. There are no absolute rules as to how long you need to grind with each pad; it's partly a matter of individual taste—how much sand and gravel you want to show—and very much a matter of grinding sufficiently and evenly across the entire surface of the countertop. Depending on the size of the piece and on how much of the fines and aggregates you want to expose, it can take several hours to go through all of the pads.

Polishing

Where "grinding" ends and "polishing" begins is somewhat a matter of personal preference. We generally quit grinding after we've used the 600-grit pad. Then we wait until the piece is about 10 days

old (but no older than 28 days) before polishing with the 800- and 1,200-grit pads. Concrete that is younger than 10 days is still too green and soft to polish well; concrete older than one month can still be polished, but the concrete is very hard at this point and polishing will demand lots of effort and lots of diamond pads.

Work with the fine pads just as you did with the coarse ones: Make sure you have an ample supply of water, that you work toward the water, and that you stop regularly to clean the surface.

When polishing our countertops, we consider the job complete once we've polished with the 1,200-grit pad. At this point, we've stopped well short of the additional steps usually taken by professional granite or marble fabricators, who polish their materials to a fine sheen using finer and finer pads as well as polishing compounds. For our purposes, however, we find this extra effort unnecessary. When polished with a 1,200-grit pad, concrete will look dull when dry, but it will feel quite smooth to the touch. It will also have enough "tooth" to help prevent a topical sealer (if used) from peeling, something these

BY THE WAY

Use wet/dry diamond sanding blocks to get into tight places, such as the soap dish on the countertop shown here, and to ease the edges.

sealers tend to do when applied to very slick surfaces (see the facing page). Sealing and waxing, we've found, give the concrete a polished look, without additional effort.

PLACING INLAYS

Most inlays are placed in the mold before the concrete is poured; they're flush with the surface of the finished piece so you can grind and polish over them. Inlays that extend above the surface, like the brass rods in the countertop featured here, must be glued in after grinding and polishing.

To glue inlays such as brass rods, use PC7 or PC11 epoxy to which pigments are added to match the color of the concrete. These glues, like all epoxies, are hard on the skin, so wear gloves. Before gluing, let the concrete dry thoroughly after grinding and polishing. This will take a day or two, depending on the weather.

Mask the surface of the countertop around the slots, and wrap three sides of each rod with more of the tape. Some of the tape on the rods will be embedded in the glue, but that's all right: It won't show.

Make a jig out of two pieces of scrap wood to help position the rods in their slots so the ends are even. Spread a thin coating of epoxy on the exposed side of each strip. Be careful not to use too much glue; ideally, there should be no excess that squeezes out when the rods

PLACING THE BRASS RODS

1. Before placing the brass rods, mask the surface of the countertop around the slots.

2. Mask three sides of each brass rod, then spread epoxy on the unmasked side. Spread the glue thinly, so as little glue as possible squeezes out of the slots when the rods are placed.

3. Push each rod firmly into its slot.

are placed. Press each rod into its slot, lining its end up against the jig.

Cut a piece of scrap MDF or ¾-in. plywood long and wide enough to cover the rods, with strips of scrap screwed along its edges, as shown in the far left photo on the facing page (these edge strips help stiffen and flatten the material). Put heavy weights on the wood to hold the rods in place while the glue sets. After the glue has hardened, peel off the masking tape and use a sharp razor to trim away any tape that might have been glued in with the rods.

SEALING THE CONCRETE

Concrete should be sealed to protect it, but the ideal sealer has yet to be invented. In choosing a sealer, you'll be making choices between two somewhat imperfect solutions: topical sealers and penetrating sealers.

Topical sealers

Topical sealers, including epoxies, urethanes, and lacquer-based and acrylic-based products, create a film over the concrete, essentially a barrier between the concrete and whatever you put or spill on it. They do a much better job than penetrating sealers of actually protecting the surface of the concrete. Thus a topical sealer may make sense for use on a countertop that is likely to get a lot of abuse from wine or vinegar or from acidic liquids like lemon juice, especially if you—or your clients—are likely to be bothered by stains from such things.

4. Use a wooden jig to position the rods so their ends are even.

5. Put a scrap of MDF or ¾-in. plywood over the rods, with bricks or other weights on top to hold the rods in place while the epoxy hardens.

▶ The countertop is ready to be sealed and waxed.

We've had good luck with lacquer-based tile sealers such as Glaze 'N Seal (see Resources on p. 195). These sealers are safe around food and relatively easy to apply, although the concrete must be completely dry before they're put on or they'll simply peel away. These sealers do a fairly good job of resisting stains, but like all topical sealers, they have a "plastic" look to them.

And that's the problem. By coating the concrete, topical sealers tend to detract from concrete's natural look. They also scratch easily and hot pots burn them, so they're not good to use around a stove. The epoxies and ure-thanes are also more difficult than pen-etrating sealers to apply correctly, and topical sealers may need to be removed— a somewhat difficult endeavor—and reapplied after a few years, depending

◀ **A topical sealer does a good job of protecting the surface of the concrete from lemon juice and other acidic liquids.**

on the level of abuse the countertop has received. Sometimes, a topical sealer will start to peel up in places, especially if the concrete's surface is very smooth; when that happens, the entire coating has to be stripped off and reapplied. And if the concrete effloresces (see "Troubleshooting" on p. 149) after the sealer has been applied, the coating will have to be stripped off, the efflorescence dealt with, and a new coat of sealer put on.

Penetrating sealers

Penetrating sealers resist stains but they don't prevent them. If you spill a glass of pinot noir on a countertop treated with a penetrating sealer or leave a lemon slice on it, you have only a couple of minutes to wipe the surface before the wine stains it or the acidic lemon juice roughens the surface. Thus you should assume that in a busy kitchen, a countertop will end up looking well used no matter how much penetrating sealer you apply.

On the up side, penetrating sealers themselves don't scratch and hot pots don't hurt them, so a penetrating sealer is good for use on a countertop by a stove. Penetrating sealers are also easy to apply: simply brush on or apply with a pad, then wipe off the excess. And maintenance is a snap—just strip the wax and reapply a few coats of sealer now and then. And unlike topical sealers, penetrating sealers don't obscure concrete's natural beauty.

For these reasons, we use penetrating sealers, followed with a coat of beeswax or carnuba wax. Penetrating sealers are either water based or solvent based. We recommend a water-based sealer for use on a countertop where food is prepared or handled (see Resources on p. 195). The following discussion on application applies only to penetrating sealers.

Other options

You might want to experiment with variations on the sealer theme. We have on occasion tried an epoxy sealer thinned with solvent; this watery epoxy acts rather like a penetrating sealer and soaks into and fills the larger pores in concrete, creating a thin barrier against stains. This barrier is not as effective as a film barrier created by thicker epoxy, but it leaves the concrete looking more natural than it would under a thick coat of epoxy.

Applying penetrating sealer and wax

To apply the sealer, you'll need a medium-width (3-in.) brush, a sponge, or a rag. You'll also need some clean rags to wipe off the excess. Use more clean rags to apply the wax, and a buffer and buffing wheel to polish it. Wear rubber gloves when working with the sealer and wax, and be sure to read the directions that come with the sealer regarding protection for your respiratory system; if you're using a solvent-based sealer, you may need a respirator-type mask rated for use around solvents.

▶ **This large countertop installation by Richard Marks has a durable, topical finish of urethane applied with his own technique.**

To apply the sealer:

1. Simply brush the sealer on liberally so that it forms puddles (there's no harm putting on too much). Cover the entire countertop at one time; don't stop for coffee and then start again or a line can appear where the earlier application joins the later one.

2. Wait about 5 min. for the sealer to soak in, then wipe off any excess with a rag that is wet with some of the sealer.

3. Apply one or two more coats of sealer after the first.

4. Wait about 45 min. for the last coat of sealer to sink in, then use a clean rag to wipe on a coat of mineral oil.

◄ ▲ Liberally brush on two or three coats of penetrating sealer. After applying each coat, wipe off the excess with a rag that's wet with some of the sealer. Wait about 5 min. before applying the next coat.

▲ Use a clean cloth to apply beeswax in areas of about 4 sq. ft. at a time. Let the wax dry for 2 min. to 3 min., then wipe off the excess with another clean cloth. Buff immediately.

▲ An automotive buffing wheel is all you need to buff out the wax.

▶ The finished surface: sealed, waxed, and buffed.

To apply the wax:

1. Apply with a clean cloth or towel.

2. Let the wax dry for 2 min. to 3 min., and then wipe off any excess with another clean cloth.

3. Buff immediately. Work in areas about 4 sq. ft. or no more than you can apply, wipe off, and buff in 2 min. to 3 min. If the wax dries longer than about 3 min., it will be difficult to buff.

TROUBLESHOOTING

A seasoned expert in concrete once remarked that there are 212 variables that must be controlled to successfully pour and finish concrete. We have on occasion reached the boiling point trying to figure out all of them. Tough as the concrete is, it can be touchy. Even the most well-planned, well-executed project can now and then go a bit awry, often for reasons that defy explanation. The good news is that there's a fix for just about every problem. Grinding and polishing will take care of most blemishes, and an epoxy filler or a slurry coat of cement and pigment can be used to fill voids and blowholes. And, when all else fails, you can always just reassemble the mold, mix up another batch of concrete, and try again. Here are the most common problems and what you can do about them.

▲ Efflorescence can usually be cleaned off with repeated washings.

Efflorescence

Efflorescence is a whitish coating of calcium-carbonate mineral salts that can form on the surface of the concrete. It's perhaps the most unpredictable—and tenaciously irritating—problem you're likely to encounter. Usually, efflorescence appears on vertical concrete structures such as retaining walls and foundations that are formed in damp locations. If moisture seeps through the concrete, it can bring with it free calcium salts in the concrete, which it deposits on the surface as it evaporates. Efflorescence can also form on a slab on grade when salts in the soil are carried up through the concrete by moisture in the ground.

Lots of things can cause efflorescence on a cast-in-mold countertop. Unfortunately, they are mostly unpredictable and often uncontrollable, such as the composition of the sand and aggregates available in your area or the ingredients in cement available at your local supplier. Also, we've found that the risk of efflorescence goes up when we work in cold weather; we're not certain why, but it could be that in the cold, there's less complete bonding of the minerals in the concrete and thus more free minerals to migrate to the surface. If you're working in the cold and you suspect efflorescence will be a problem (if you've poured samples that effloresced, for example), try working in a heated space if you can. We've also noticed that efflorescence is more likely to form on vertical pieces such as kitchen islands and room divides.

We first encountered the problem of efflorescence on our fourth countertop, a huge, 20-ft.-long, very ambitious, very black piece—a piece for which we spent two months and several thousand dollars making the mold. It turned completely and utterly white as it cured. We spent a long time trying to figure out what happened on that one and called several people in the industry. "Well, it effloresced," they told us, without a great deal of sympathy, "welcome to the club." We spent five days and five nights leaching the piece with water. Fortunately, after the fifth day and lots of grinding, we had a black countertop again and a happy client.

So, before you commit lots of your time and financial resources to a big project, make some samples using local materials to see what happens. If you get efflorescence, try using a different brand of cement—a high lime or gypsum content in the cement may be the cause—or sand and aggregates from a different source.

To clean off efflorescence, wash the piece with water repeatedly. The process may take several days as you wash off one layer of salts, then wait to see if another forms. Fortunately, the process will be finite—there is only a limited amount of soluble salts in a concrete countertop, and repeated washings will eventually leach out all of them.

Water stains, dull spots, ghosting, and other blemishes

Water stains on the finished surface of a piece occur when water pools in the bottom of the mold during curing. Dull, discolored areas on the surface are another common problem. They form when water leaks out of the freshly poured concrete, typically through a

BY THE WAY

Don't apply a topical sealer to a countertop that has effloresced until you're quite sure the process has stopped; if it hasn't, the sealer will seal in any additional deposits that form. The sealer will have to be removed so the new efflorescence can be washed off.

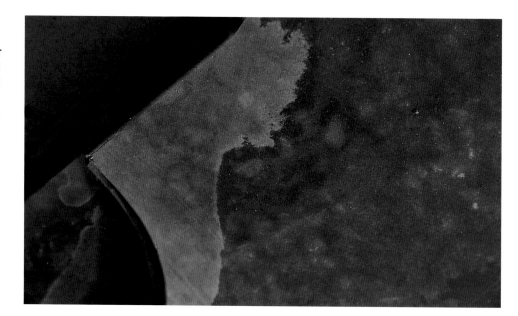

▶ Discolorations like this can occur when water pools in the mold or when the mold leaks, allowing water to seep out of the concrete as it's curing. Such stains can be ground and polished out.

Ghosting occurs when the reinforcing rods are too close to the surface. It sometimes goes away as the concrete cures. It can't be ground or polished out if it doesn't disappear, but grinding to expose the aggregate will help obscure the marks.

pinhole in the mold along a seam that wasn't completely caulked or through a scratch or gouge in the mold material that's deep enough for water to seep through. Fortunately, blemishes from water stains or leaks in the mold can be polished out.

Ghosting is less common and occurs when the reinforcing materials are placed—or dislodged during the pour—so they're too close to the surface of the concrete. This causes a slight change in the color of the concrete directly over the reinforcing material. Ghosting may fade with time as the concrete continues to cure, though not always. Ghosting that doesn't fade can't be polished out, but grinding to expose the aggregates tends to obscure it; ghosting is simply less noticeable against a varied background.

Cracks

There's an old saying: "If it ain't cracked, it ain't concrete." As mentioned previously, some crazing—small surface cracks—is very common, and we actually welcome the effect. Large cracks are another matter. Properly mixed and cured concrete shouldn't develop big cracks like those in the photo on p. 152. Such large cracks usually occur when the mix has too much water in it or when water is allowed to evaporate out of the concrete to such a degree that the concrete can't properly hydrate. These cracks indicate excess shrinkage and possibly weakening of the concrete.

Of course, weakened concrete may not be a problem if the piece is well supported, but large cracks are unsightly. At first glance, a big crack can be demoralizing. But with skillful use of patching and grinding, it's quite possible to "save" what had seemed a disaster. Fill cracks with a mixture of PC7 (or PC11) epoxy and pigment to match the concrete's color. Apply with a putty knife and sand lightly when hardened.

▶ Big cracks like this are usually a sign of excessive shrinkage as the concrete cured. Fill with epoxy colored to match the concrete, and sand flat when the glue has hardened.

Voids and other woes

They're commonly referred to as bug-holes, blowholes, honeycombing, and voids—or sometimes in less polite terms. Whatever you call them, they're holes in the concrete's surface, and they can be either an aggravation or an opportunity—it's a matter of perspective. A few small holes in the surface may not be a problem at all, depending on how the piece will be used. You certainly don't want holes in the surface of a kitchen sink run, but a few holes in a fireplace mantel or a vertical room divide, for example, could be viewed as desirable—expressions of the essential nature of the material, rather than flaws.

Some fabricators, such as Buddy Rhodes, deliberately create voids in their finished concrete, which they fill with a cement and pigment mix that has a slightly different color from the original piece, creating an intricate, attractive texture in the surface coloring.

The countertop used as an example in this book came out of the mold with a number of small holes throughout its surface. They weren't intentional. These holes probably resulted from insufficient vibration, from a mix that had too little slump, or both. Concrete contains a lot of air, which forms bubbles when poured. These bubbles get trapped against the sides of the mold. When you vibrate the concrete, as noted in the previous chapter, these bubbles should break free and rise to the surface to escape. If you don't vibrate the concrete long enough—or if your vibrator isn't up to the job—some of the bubbles may remain, and the concrete hardens around them, causing the small holes. If

◀ Lots of things can cause holes in the surface of the concrete, including insufficient vibration or a mix that's not wet enough. Small holes are easily fixed with colored epoxy; for lots of larger holes, use a slurry of cement paste and pigment.

the concrete is too stiff or too tacky—typically because there is too much sand in the mix—no vibration will be sufficient to dislodge all the bubbles. Also, lightweight aggregates—which are more porous that regular aggregate—hold more air, which tends to produce more bubbles and the potential for more holes.

Holes in the concrete can also result when the cement mortar doesn't completely fill the spaces between aggregates. These holes are often larger than those caused by air bubbles, and they tend to be more irregular in shape. Insufficient vibration is the most likely cause of such voids. Other possible causes are a mix that's too stiff or a mix that doesn't contain enough cement or

fines. Whatever the cause, such voids are easily repaired, and, again, the fix itself provides a design opportunity.

For a few small holes, we'll use PC7 (or PC11) epoxy and pigment to match the original concrete. We apply and smooth the fill with a putty knife, then lightly sand with a fine wet/dry sandpaper.

Because the piece used here as an example had many holes as well as a few small chips in the concrete around the brass rods, we mixed a slurry of cement, pigment, and water reducer to fill them. We didn't add sand to the slurry because we wanted a very fine mixture that would fill the smallest voids. We applied this fill in the same manner that grout is applied to tile.

BY THE WAY

With all the variables inherent in pouring concrete, it is inevitable that the unexpected may occur. On many occasions, we have learned to make "lemonade from lemons." Rather than discard an entire countertop in pursuit of perfection, we have learned that the cure is sometimes worth the disease, and an entire method of achieving a new look can be the result of an accident. Tile pieces can be applied as mosaic into a void, grinding irregularities into the surface can "reveal" colorful aggregate, and concrete acid-based color stains can adjust for poor color resolution.

Applying the slurry

To fill the holes and chipouts using a slurry coat, use the same brand of cement you used for the main piece, if you want the best chance of a color match.

1. Measure the cement by weight because you'll use that figure to calculate pigments and water reducer. For a piece like the one shown here—a typical size, lots of small holes—use 2 lb. or 3 lb. of cement. That's probably more cement than you'll need, but you definitely want too much rather than too little.

2. Add pigments in the same proportions used to color the concrete (0.7 percent black and 8 percent blue, in the example here), if you want the fills to match. But again, sometimes fills of a slightly different shade create interesting effects.

3. Use water reducer at the recommended maximum amount, by weight of the cement.

4. Add only enough water to create a mix with a thick, somewhat gelatinous consistency, like that of toothpaste.

▲ To make a slurry to fill holes in the surface of the concrete, add pigments to the cement as a percentage of the cement weight. Mix pigments in the same proportions used for the main piece, if you want the fills to match.

▲ Use the maximum amount of water reducer and only enough water to create a mix with a thick, gelatinous consistency. This helps prevent shrinkage, making a secure bond between the fills and the concrete.

◄ Thoroughly wet the surface of the concrete before applying the slurry. Dry concrete will absorb water out of the slurry and make it hard to spread.

◄ Spread the slurry with a broad putty knife, working it back and forth as you would when applying tile grout.

5. Before applying the slurry, thoroughly moisten the surface of the countertop; dry concrete will suck water out of the slurry, making it hard to spread. Keep a spray bottle handy and spray the countertop and slurry frequently as you work. Don't let the slurry get too wet, though; too much water will weaken the slurry.

6. Put a handful of the slurry on the countertop. Use a broad-bladed putty knife to apply a thick coat to an area only as large as you can handle comfortably. Working quickly, spread the coating back and forth, as you would when applying tile grout, to be sure the mix completely fills all of the holes. Spray the coating frequently

▶ It's all right to run the slurry over inlays.

▶ Scrape off excess slurry as you work, and use a wet sponge to wipe off any film that's left.

to keep it wet enough to work. Thoroughly scrape off all excess slurry as you work, and use a sponge that's been rinsed in clean water to wipe off any film that's left.

7. Use a narrower (about 1-in.) putty knife to work around insets such as brass rods. Keep the knife as flat as possible when filling large voids like chipouts; you want to float in an

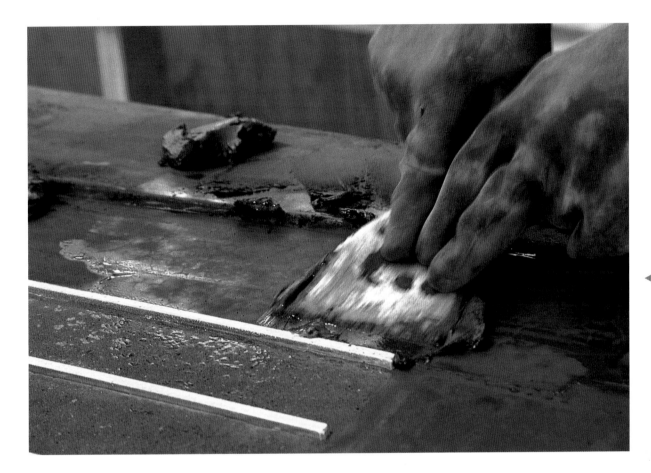

◀ This countertop had a few chips along the edges of the slots for the rods. With the rods in place, we worked some of the slurry into the chips with a narrow putty knife.

even, smooth fill. Be careful not to let the knife blade dip into the soft slurry.

8. Let the fills cure for about 3 days, then sand lightly using very fine wet/dry sandpaper with a sanding block or palm sander. You'll find that it doesn't take a lot of polishing to smooth the fills and remove any excess slurry that has dried onto the countertop.

BY THE WAY

Use a light solution (2 percent to 5 percent) of muriatic acid or vinegar to sponge off the slurry coat film (just as tilesetters do when washing out grout-film buildup).

INSTALLING THE COUNTERTOP

Installing a concrete countertop requires some brains, of course, but also a good deal of brawn. Remember that concrete made with regular aggregates weighs about 140 lb. per cu. ft. The countertop discussed here and throughout in the book is fairly typical in terms of weight: It contains about 3 cu. ft. and weighs a respectable 420 lb., or about 210 lb. for each of its two sections.

It's a good idea to have two or three fairly stout helpers on hand to safely finesse the sections of your countertop into place. While a couple hundred pounds itself isn't necessarily a lot of weight, in the form of a section of countertop, it's an awkward 200 lb. And if your countertop, like this one, has long, narrow arms around a sink knockout, then it's also a somewhat fragile 200 lb. The more hands you have to handle each piece, the easier the countertop will be to install safely. That's assuming your helpers don't get in each other's way, of course—talk through each move before making it, then assign one person to give directions during the move.

PREPARING THE CABINETS

Ideally, you will have purchased, reinforced, and installed your cabinets before making the mold for the countertop; the way in which you reinforce the cabinets can change their dimensions and their position when installed, and thus can affect the dimensions

▶ Off-the-shelf modular cabinets like these need to be reinforced. The thin back panel can be strengthened with a ½-in. sheet of plywood, glued and screwed in place. A single sheet of ¾-in. plywood on top will help spread the weight of the heavy countertop.

or wood-veneer doors and drawer fronts. The cabinets are reasonably priced, attractive, functional, and quite adequate for a typical countertop of Corian, Formica, or even marble or granite of standard thickness. But such cabinets are a bit too flimsy for a 2½-in.-thick concrete countertop and need to be reinforced.

To beef up the two cabinets—a 36-in. sink bay and a 12-in. base cabinet next to it—that would support the counter-top shown here, we reinforced the back panels, base, and top.

Reinforcing the back panels

The ¼-in. fiberboard back panels of the cabinets were set into a ¼-in. rabbet in the bottom and sides and in the back stretcher along the top. We removed these panels and used wood glue and a few small finish nails to fasten a panel of ½-in. plywood to each, creating ¾-in.-thick panels. Using a copy bit and router, we deepened the rabbets to accommodate the thicker panels, then screwed and glued them in place. These ¾-in. panels helped to stiffen the cabi-nets and keep them square and helped transfer the weight of the countertop to the floor.

Reinforcing the base

We discarded the adjustable plastic legs that came with the cabinets. The legs are entirely suitable for a relatively lightweight countertop, but they're not sturdy enough to support a heavy con-crete countertop.

To replace the legs, we built kick-frames of doubled-up ¾-in. plywood

BY THE WAY

When choosing off-the-shelf cabi-nets that will need to be rein-forced, be sure that a thickened back panel can be fully set into the cabinet frame: Depending on a cabinet's design, hardware or shelving may get in the way. If a thickened back panel can't be installed flush with the back of the cabinet, be sure that there's room around the cabinet for any of the panel that extends out and that you can trim out or otherwise hide the exposed paneling. Also, be sure that there is still ample room within the cabinet—after the new panel has been installed—for such things as faucet hardware and the sink.

of the countertop and how it fits on the cabinets.

We generally install our countertops on custom-made cabinets. These are solid boxes made with ¾-in. plywood on the sides, back, and top. They easily handle the extra weight of a concrete countertop and don't need to be reinforced.

Our client on the job highlighted here chose a popular style of off-the-shelf modular cabinet. This type of cabi-net typically has fiberboard sides and a fiberboard bottom, an open top with narrow fiberboard stretchers across the front and back, a ¼-in. fiberboard back panel, adjustable plastic legs, and wood

▲ Plan ahead to be sure there's room for the ½-in. plywood reinforcing panel. In this case, the hardware used to fasten together the cabinets prevented the panel from being set flush with the back—a typical situation. Fortunately, there was room for it, and the panel's exposed edge was hidden by a dishwasher.

▲ Modular cabinets sometimes come with adjustable plastic legs and clip-on toe-kicks. Replace them with a wooden frame, shimmed to level.

strips and faced the front of each with the ¾-in. fiberboard and wood veneer toekick material that came with the cabinets. Such frames create a strong support for the cabinets and help to distribute the weight of the countertop over a wide area.

Because the floor under the cabinets had a rather extreme slope—more than 1 in. in 8 ft.—we cut long shims and put them under the kickframes to create

a level surface on which to place the cabinets. Since the toekick is held back from the front of the cabinet, the change in elevation from left to right is not noticeable.

We screwed and glued the strips and shims together, and secured the frame in position with blocks of wood screwed to the floor at the corners.

Reinforcing the top

We cut a single piece of ABX plywood to cover the tops of the cabinets and to extend across the dishwasher bay on the left and to a ledger of doubled-up ¾-in. plywood screwed to the wall on the right. We fastened it in place temporarily with a couple of drywall screws.

When fastened permanently, this top panel will spread the weight of the countertop more evenly over the cabinets. It will also create a flat, level substrate for the countertop. After installation, we faced the exposed edge of the plywood top panel with zinc (see p. 172).

▲ Doubled-up ¾-in. plywood, screwed to the end wall, carries one end of the countertop where there's no supporting cabinet. A 1½-in.-thick ledger lag-bolted into the studs could substitute for the plywood.

▲ Adding a ¾-in. plywood top panel spreads the weight of the countertop more evenly over the cabinets and also creates a flat, level substrate for the countertop.

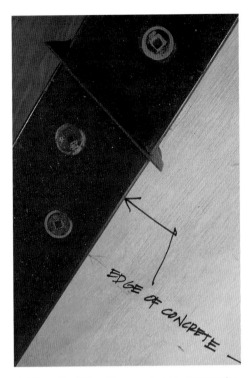

▲ When dry fitting the countertop, protect the delicate edges with a little foam padding.

◄ The "dry fit" lets you make sure that the counter-top fits on the cabinets as planned, that the overhang is even, and that voids for such things as the faucet and air gap have been positioned properly.

INSTALLING THE COUNTERTOP

Installation of a countertop like the one featured here, with an undermounted sink, has three distinct phases: dry fitting, mounting the sink, and the actual installation.

Dry fitting the countertop

Set up some sawhorses close to the cabinets. Place the sections of the countertop on the sawhorses during the "dry fit." This will save you and your crew from a lot of heavy lifting. If your countertop, like the one shown here, has long, narrow arms around a sink knockout, be sure to support them properly (see p. 133).

Carefully place each section of the countertop on the plywood substrate. If your countertop has a diagonal divide like the piece shown here, be careful pushing the two sections together; the sharp corners formed by the acute angles at the ends of the sections around the sink knockout are easily chipped. We used scraps of thin foam padding to protect them.

Check the countertop's overhang and position over the sink bay. This dry fit lets you make sure, one last time, that everything fits as planned: for example, that the faucet knockouts in the countertop coincide with the plumbing and that the countertop rests flat on the cabinets.

With the countertop in its final position, trace the sink opening on the plywood substrate that covers the cabinets.

With the countertop in its final position, trace the sink knockout on the plywood substrate. Remove the countertop, and place the sections on the sawhorses. This line will help determine where and how the sink will be mounted.

Mounting the sink

There are a couple ways to position and mount a sink. One is to fasten the sink directly against the underside of the countertop using tapcons (special screws designed for concrete) and large steel washers or mounting clips supplied with the sink (see the drawing at left below). The other method is the one we use here.

Our client wanted a custom-made sink as large as would fit in the sink bay. As a result, when in place, the sides of the sink would be only 1 in. from the sides of the cabinet bay, which would not leave enough room to mount the sink from beneath using the tapcons and washers. In such a situation, the sink's flange rests on top of the substrate (or on top of the cabinet walls if there is no solid substrate). The sink is secured to the substrate with silicone caulk. The countertop will then rest on top of the flange, and the joint is sealed with more caulk.

Measure back ¼ in. all around the line that marks the countertop's sink knockout on the substrate. This second line defines the opening in the substrate for the sink, which mounts beneath a ¼-in. overhang. Drill starter

Mounting the Sink with Tapcons

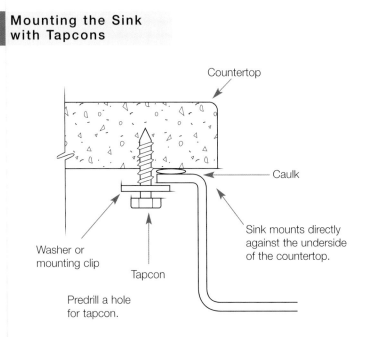

Countertop

Caulk

Washer or mounting clip

Tapcon

Sink mounts directly against the underside of the countertop.

Predrill a hole for tapcon.

Mounting the Sink on Substrate

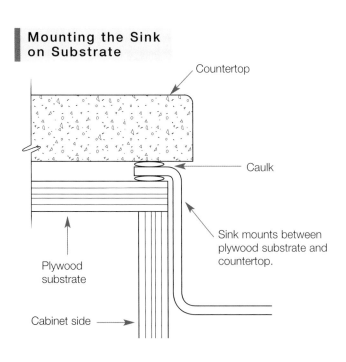

Countertop

Caulk

Sink mounts between plywood substrate and countertop.

Plywood substrate

Cabinet side

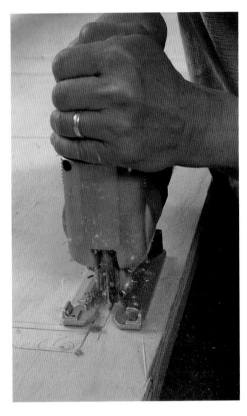

To make a hole in the substrate for the sink, drill starter holes in the corners, then cut with a jigsaw. To accommodate an overhang—¼ in., in this case—cut ¼ in. outside the line traced to mark the actual sink opening.

holes at each corner of the line marking the sink opening, and use a jigsaw to cut out the piece. Notch out openings for the faucet and air-gap hardware.

Place the sink in the opening in the plywood substrate and check that it fits properly (see the photo at right on p. 166). Sinks sometimes have irregularities that have to be fixed on the spot. In this case, the flange had a slight bow in it, which we hammered out.

Put a section of the countertop back in place and check its fit on the sink. Then place the other section against it, checking the overhangs over the front of the cabinets and over the sink, as well as the alignment of the two sections and the position of the faucet

and air-gap knockouts over the holes in the substrate.

Remove the countertop, and trace a line on the substrate around the sink flange. Remove the sink, and run a bead of caulk along the edge of the sink opening in the substrate inside the line marking the edge of the flange. Replace the sink, and press it into the caulk (see the photo essay on pp. 168–169).

Clean the sink with denatured alcohol to remove any grease left on the steel after manufacturing, then mask the top of the sink with tape. Also, mask the bottom edge of the countertop's sink knockout and around the ends of the sink knockout's arms in both sections.

▲ Notch the substrate to accommodate the hardware for the faucet and air gap.

▲ Place the sink in the opening to check that it fits. Trace a line around the outside edge of the sink flange.

Final installation

Apply a generous amount of caulk (or construction adhesive) to half of the substrate and along half of the sink flange. Lower one section of the countertop into place.

Apply more caulk to the other half of the substrate and sink flange. Place the other section carefully on the substrate. As much as possible, lower both sections directly into place so you don't have to slide them into position.

Push the two sections together, checking the alignment again. You should see the caulk squeeze up between the sections as they come together. Leave the caulk for now; after it dries, it can be easily cut away with a razor.

If you have a couple of long pipe clamps, place them lengthwise on a blanket or other padding on the countertop, and use them to pull the two sections tightly together; caulk

▲ ▶ With the sink temporarily in place, put the countertop in place to check the fit, the overhang, and the alignment of the two sections.

1. Run a bead of silicone caulk around the edge of the sink opening in the substrate, inside the line marking the edge of the sink flange.

2. Lower the sink into place, and press it into the caulk.

3. Before final placement of the countertop, mask the top edge of the sink, the bottom edge of the sink opening in the countertop, and the ends of the countertop's narrow arms that surround the sink.

4. Apply a generous amount of silicone caulk (construction adhesive can be used instead) to half of the substrate.

5. Caulk along half of the sink flange.

6. Carefully lower one section of the countertop onto the caulk.

7. Check the alignment at the back . . .

8. . . . and at the front.

▲ Apply a generous amount of caulk to the ends of the arms that surround the sink opening.

▲ When you push the two sections of countertop together, caulk should ooze out of the joint. It can be trimmed with a razor after it has dried.

◄ If possible, use bar clamps to pull the sections together (be sure to pad the countertop). Using clamps this way may not be possible if one or both ends of the countertop are butted against a wall. Here, the left end of the countertop was open, and the other stopped 6 in. short of the wall to make space for a small slate shelf.

should squeeze out of the joint. We used three linked, 4-ft. bar clamps. We also used a pair of C-clamps, cushioned with scrap plywood, to align the front seam where the two sections joined. This helped create a smooth junction in the front. We also clamped the front edge of each section with one C-clamp cushioned with a scrap of plywood.

Leave the clamps in place for at least 12 hr. After removing the clamps, peel off the making tape and use a razor to clean off any caulk that squeezed out between the joints.

INSTALLING THE BACKSPLASH

Backsplashes for a concrete countertop can be made of any number of materials: tile, glass, stainless steel, copper. For this countertop, we decided to use Chinese green slate. The slate came in 12-in. squares, which varied widely in color and texture. We felt that whole squares were too large in proportion to the setting, so we cut the squares into 3-in. strips using a tile saw. These smaller pieces created varied blocks of

USING TAPCONS TO FASTEN A COUNTERTOP

▲ **A few tapcons (screws made for use in concrete) help to ensure that the countertop won't shift. Tapcons are self-tapping, but it's a good idea to predrill with a masonry bit. Place one tapcon for every square foot.**

A layer of caulk or construction adhesive alone is sufficient to keep a heavy concrete countertop in place under most circumstances. However, an unfastened, free-standing concrete countertop, especially one in a busy area such as a kitchen, could shift if enough people happen to lean against it at the same time. Such shifting can damage the countertop, especially if it has a diagonal divide with easily chipped sharp corners.

As a matter of routine practice, we fasten all of our countertops with tapcons in addition to caulk or construction adhesive. Most of our countertops are installed in the San Francisco Bay Area—which means an occasional earthquake can occur. A quake strong enough to bounce around an unfastened concrete countertop is likely to cause so many more serious problems that a little movement of a countertop will be a minor concern, but a countertop that is well fastened with caulk or adhesive and tapcons will likely remain in place—even if nothing else does—and that means one less thing to worry about.

Tapcons (see Resources on p. 195) are hardened screws made especially for use in concrete. When there's a plywood substrate under the countertop, we generally use one tapcon for each square foot of countertop. They're easy to install: Using a masonry bit, predrill through the substrate into the bottom of the countertop. Mix up a little PC7 epoxy, and dip the tip of each tapcon in the glue and simply screw into place.

▲ **Before installing the tapcons, dip the end of each in PC7 epoxy.**

---

color and texture that were more in scale with the surroundings.

We'll sometimes install the countertop directly against the studs, then bring the cementboard underlayment for the backsplash down onto a bed of caulk run along the back edge of the countertop. In this case, we installed the cementboard first, then butted the countertop against it.

Before installing the backsplash, run a bead of silicone caulk along the junction of the cementboard and countertop. Here, we applied the slate strips randomly in a running pattern in a bed of thinset, as we would tiles. Once the mortar had cured, we wiped a coat of marine acrylic onto the slate. We like to apply another coat of beeswax once the backsplash has been installed (see chapter 5).

Before finishing the raw edge of the plywood substrate, run a bead of caulk along the seam between the top edge of the plywood and the bottom of the countertop. This bead provides protection against any water that might run down the front of the countertop and

Backsplash Detail

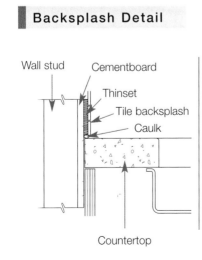

Wall stud
Cementboard
Thinset
Tile backsplash
Caulk
Countertop

1. Caulk the seam between the countertop and the exposed front edge of the plywood substrate.

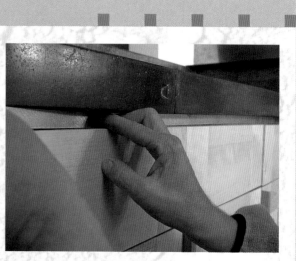

2. Place a strip of galvanized metal (here, zinc) against the front edge.

3. Use a piece of scrap wood and a small mallet to seat the strip into the caulk.

4. The finished edge.

along the underside to the substrate. You can use any number of materials to finish the raw edge. We often use a strip of black plastic laminate, glued on with construction adhesive. In this case, because the countertops placed perpendicular to the concrete were covered with zinc, we use a strip of zinc on the substrate. Set back beneath the countertop, the zinc strip is barely noticeable, but it's a nice detail when seen from a distance.

▲ **The finished countertop.**

APPENDIX 1

BUILDING A CURVED FORM

The curved form truly takes advantage of the "moldability" of concrete. Although the mold is a bit more difficult to build, it is well worth the effort. There are many ways to make a curved form. Shown here is one of the simplest (see the drawing on the facing page).

Note that this method assumes that the mold bottom has not been cut to size but rather is a full sheet of melamine, with the sides of the mold mounted on top of the mold bottom and supported with backer boards.

1. If you used a template and defined the curved portion of the finished countertop with the template, transfer this curve to a piece of ¾-in. exterior-grade plywood. If you did not use a template, simply strike the arc to define the curve directly onto the plywood.

2. Calculate the total thickness of the combined materials you'll use to form the curved portion of the mold. In this case: two ¼-in. pieces of Masonite and a ⅛₆-in. piece of plastic laminate, a total of ⅚₆ in.

3. Use a compass as a gauge to scribe ⅚₆ in. to the outside of the first curve. You now have two arcs. The inner arc is the finished surface of the mold (and thus of the countertop). The outer arc marks the cut in the plywood.

4. Using a jigsaw, cut along the scribed outer line. Square both ends of the arc where the curved portion of the mold will tie into the straight sides. Trace the arc on a second sheet of plywood and cut.

5. Fasten one piece of plywood to the mold bottom with drywall screws. Use spacers wide enough to hold the top of the second sheet up to roughly the depth of the finished countertop. Fasten the second sheet and the spacers to the first.

6. Cut two strips of ¼-in. Masonite exactly the depth of the finished countertop. Press each piece of Masonite into the plywood frame, mark the ends, and cut so it's flush with the ends of the arc.

7. Screw and glue the first Masonite strip to the plywood frame. Glue and clamp the second strip to the first.

8. Cut a strip of ¹⁄₁₆-in. plastic laminate (P-Lam) the same width as the Masonite, leaving it long. Press the P-Lam against the Masonite, and mark and trim the ends so they are flush.

9. Brush contact cement onto the surfaces of both the Masonite and the P-Lam. Let it dry per the directions. Starting at one end, carefully press the P-Lam into place.

10. To continue the sides of the mold with straight pieces of ¾-in. melamine, butt them against the ends of the curved form, their inside surfaces flush with the surface of the curved section. Support them with backer boards.

11. Caulk all seams with black silicone caulk.

Curved Form

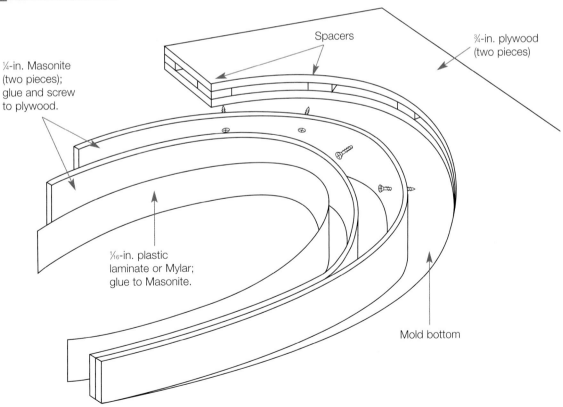

Spacers

¾-in. plywood (two pieces)

¼-in. Masonite (two pieces); glue and screw to plywood.

¹⁄₁₆-in. plastic laminate or Mylar; glue to Masonite.

Mold bottom

APPENDIX 2

FORMING A DROP-DOWN FRONT EDGE

A drop-down front edge gives a sense of mass to the overall countertop without much added weight. This is an effective design device that accentuates an earthy, stonelike quality and works harmoniously with concrete.

To create a drop-down front edge:

1. Cut one length of melamine as wide as the front face of the drop-down front edge (labeled A in the drawing on the facing page) and as long as the countertop.

2. Bevel one edge of this piece so it creates a slight angle back (in this case, 83 degrees, or 7 degrees off square).

3. Cut a second length (B) that is as wide as A minus the depth of the rest of the countertop. For example, for a 2½-in. countertop with a 6-in. drop-down front edge, B would be 3½ in. wide. Put a 45-degree angle on the bottom edge of B. This angle will create room so you can trowel close to the corner of the drop-down edge as you finish the bottom of the countertop during the pour.

4. Assemble the mold as usual, but place the sides on top of the mold bottom and support them with backer boards.

5. Place rebar as you would normally but curve the crosspieces up into what will become the drop-down edge. Hold them back toward the center of the dropped edge. Run a piece of rebar the length of the countertop about 2 in. from the "top" and tie it to the vertical pieces. Hang the rebar from the top edge of the mold.

6. Cut gussets (C) out of ¾-in. plywood as shown in the drawing. Make enough to place one gusset every 12 in. along the length of the mold.

BY THE WAY

Standard appliances such as dishwashers and undercounter refrigerators create height restrictions in the overall height from floor to counter. Calculate the overall height of the appliance in question, add the height of the drop-down edge you want, and see if the final height works for you.

Drop-Down Edge Form

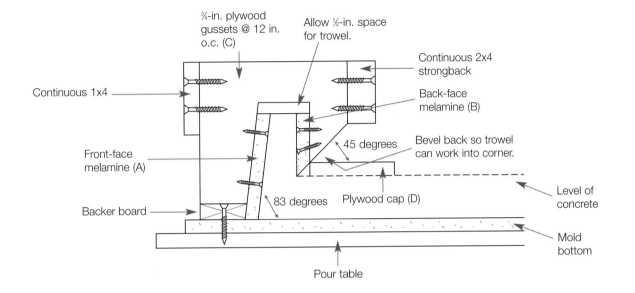

¾-in. plywood gussets @ 12 in. o.c. (C)

Allow ½-in. space for trowel.

Continuous 2x4 strongback

Continuous 1x4

Back-face melamine (B)

Front-face melamine (A)

45 degrees

Bevel back so trowel can work into corner.

Backer board

83 degrees

Plywood cap (D)

Level of concrete

Mold bottom

Pour table

Put a 45-degree angle on the back edge of each gusset as shown. The gussets fit over the mold and hold B in place.

7. Screw the gussets to the backer board and to B. Fasten a 2x4 strongback to the gussets as shown.

8. When pouring the concrete, fill the main part of the mold first. Vibrate the concrete, then screed and trowel the surface.

9. Fill the upraised portion that forms the edge and vibrate the concrete again. The weight of the concrete in this raised portion may cause the concrete below it to bulge out if the mix has too much slump. But more likely, by the time the concrete in the main part of the countertop has been poured, vibrated, and screeded, it will have stiffened up enough so that this won't happen. If it does,

scrape the bulge flat and fasten down a ¾-in. by 12-in. piece of plywood (D) the length of the countertop to act as a cap. Add enough additional concrete to fill the edge to the top of the mold, then vibrate again.

10. Screed the edge between each gusset with a short piece of wood, then trowel it smooth. Remember that this edge will be visible from the front, so be sure the mold is filled completely and that the concrete is troweled to create a smooth edge.

APPENDIX 3

POURING A COUNTERTOP IN PLACE

Pouring a countertop in place has certain advantages over the cast-in-mold approach described in this book. For one thing, the form for a poured-in-place countertop is relatively simple to make. And you don't have to worry about finding a place to set up shop or moving the heavy pieces once they've cured because the pour and installation take place simultaneously. And curing is a simple operation if the place where you pour your poured-in-place countertop happens to be in a heated room. All these advantages also apply to pouring hearths and interior floor slabs.

However, the poured-in-place approach has several drawbacks, and from our perspective, some of these are significant. First, the technique places significant limits on design: Artful changes in the surface of the countertop, such as inlays or an integral drainboard or undermounted sink, become

very difficult (though not impossible) to include.

Second, troweling to create a flat, smooth surface requires considerable skill; it's something that should be attempted only by someone who has had experience finishing concrete. In fact, a cast-in-mold countertop, though arguably a more ambitious project in many ways, is better suited to the skills of a beginner. However, even if your concrete finishing skills are somewhat lacking, you can always grind and polish the surface of a poured-in-place countertop just as you would a cast-in-mold piece, as described in chapter 5. Which brings us to a third problem with poured-in-place countertops: Pouring concrete is a messy operation under any circumstance, and the process of grinding and polishing is, if anything, even messier. Thus we like to work outdoors if possible, or at least in our shop, not in a client's kitchen.

▶ This fireplace surround was poured in place using the same techniques as for a poured-in-place countertop.

However, if you're experienced with concrete, you or your client are tolerant of the mess, you're not intent on lots of design elements, and you'd like to try a poured-in-place piece, we suggest you use techniques developed by our friend Al Jeeves. Al, a concrete contractor in the Bay Area—he's the founder and owner of Aussie-Crete— learned his craft in Australia. He takes a direct, no-nonsense approach to completing a pour.

Many of the basics concerning planning and design; mixing and pouring; curing; and grinding, polishing, and sealing outlined elsewhere in this book apply to a poured-in-place countertop, so review the relevant chapters before continuing. And most important, check that the cabinets on which the countertop will be poured, and the floor under the cabinets, are sturdy enough to support the weight. Reinforce the cabinets and floor joists if necessary.

CONCRETE MIX

For the countertop shown here, which he poured in his own kitchen, Al Jeeves ordered a full yard of 6-sack readymix with ¾-in. aggregate, water reducer, and 2 lb. of Davis Colors plum-colored pigment per sack of cement. A yard of concrete was much more than he needed for the countertop, so Al used the leftovers to make a hearth for a fireplace in the living room. If you prefer, use the mix recipe described in chapter 3 and follow the directions for mixing and pouring outlined in chapter 4.

BUILDING THE FORM

To make the bottom of the countertop, cover the cabinet boxes with ½-in. Durock, a cementboard typically used as backing for tile (see Resources on p. 195). The board won't warp as wood can under a load of wet mix, and its rough surface makes a good bond with the concrete. Hold the Durock back from the edge of the cabinet boxes about ¼ in. and bevel the edge back just slightly. Fasten the Durock to the top of the cabinet boxes with deck screws. Once the concrete has bonded to the Durock, the entire structure—cabinets, Durock, and countertop—will be virtually unmovable.

To create a small overhang along the front of the cabinets, and to hide the edge of the Durock, clamp a length of 1⅛-in. CDX plywood along the front of the cabinet frame, positioning the spacer so its top edge is even with the top of the frame (see the drawing on p. 182). For the side of the form, screw a 4-in. length of CDX to the spacer. The width of this strip will define the depth of the countertop. Here, Al went for a 4-in.-thick countertop, which gave it a substantial profile and placed the countertop 38 in. above the floor, a height he prefers over the standard 36 in.

To keep water in the concrete from leaking out of the form and running down over the cabinet boxes, run a length of plastic masking tape (duct tape also works well) along the spacer

▶ Cover the cabinet boxes with ½-in. cementboard to make the bottom of the countertop.

To create the sides of the form, clamp (or screw) a length of CDX plywood along the front of the cabinet frame.

Bevel the front edge of the cementboard.

and up the side of the form. Tape all other seams in the same way.

This countertop has a 10-in. cantilever at one end. To create a cantilever, build a box using ¾-in. CDX plywood for the sides and a sheet of MDF covered with plastic laminate (melamine, for example) for the bottom. Place the top of this laminate even with the bottom of the Durock. This forms a lip

that will cover the Durock when the countertop is poured. Seal the seam between the laminate and the Durock with more plastic masking tape. Support the box with several 2x4s, as shown in the photos on p. 182.

Form the sink knockout with 2x4s. Al's knockout was exactly the same size as the sink itself. If you choose to create a slight overhang of ¼ in. or ½ in., sim-

Creating an Overhang

CDX plywood spacer

Height of countertop

CDX plywood screwed or clamped to spacer

Durock cementboard

Cabinet-frame front

Spacers determine depth of overhang.

▲ ▶ **To create a cantilever (shown above), build a box using ¾-in. CDX plywood for the sides and a sheet of MDF covered with plastic laminate for the bottom. Support the cantilever with a framework of 2x4s.**

ply make the knockout slightly smaller than the sink. Round the corners of the knockout with a jigsaw, and wrap it with more of the plastic masking tape. Don't fasten the knockout in place yet.

To create an edge that hides the Durock around the opening for the sink, and to allow an undermounted

sink to attach directly to the concrete, Al has devised a simple and quite ingenious solution:

1. If you have a template for your sink, place the template on the Durock and mark the sink's exact size and location.

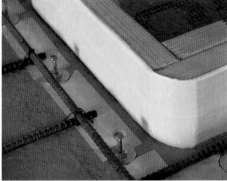

▲ Form the sink knockout with 2x4s, round the corners with a jigsaw, and wrap the assembly with plastic masking tape.

▲ Drill holes around the edge of the cutout, and place the mounting bolts for the sink.

2. Measure out from there 1 in. all around. Cut along this line using a jigsaw, and remove the cutout.

3. To place the mounting hardware for the sink, drill holes around the edge of the cutout, and place the mounting bolts as shown in the photo at right above.

4. Position the sink knockout on the cutout, and fasten it from beneath with a few deck screws.

5. Put the entire assembly in place, supporting it from beneath with 2x4s.

6. Tape the seam with plastic masking tape.

Once the concrete sets up, you can remove the knockout to trowel and finish the top and edges of the countertop, but leave the Durock cutout in place for at least one week while the concrete cures and hardens, to make sure the mounting hardware for the sink is held securely. After a week, remove the supports and slide the cutout down and off the bolts. Once the sink is bolted in place, it will hide the Durock.

Creating an Edge around the Sink Opening

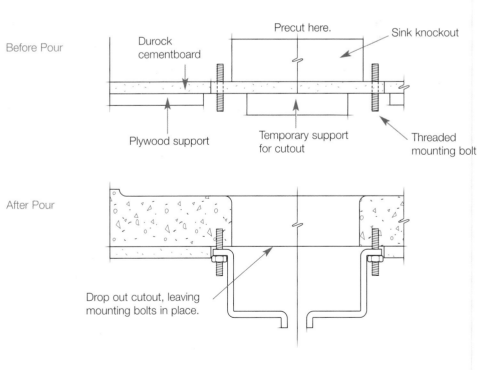

Before Pour

Durock cementboard

Precut here.

Sink knockout

Plywood support

Temporary support for cutout

Threaded mounting bolt

After Pour

Drop out cutout, leaving mounting bolts in place.

▲ Use a length of 1¼-in. PVC pipe to make a knockout for the faucet.

► Wire together a grid of ⅜-in. rebar on 6-in. centers to reinforce the concrete.

To make a knockout for the faucet, Al used a length of 1¼-in. (inside diameter) PVC pipe, which he cut out with a reciprocating saw once the concrete had hardened. (If there's a dishwasher under the counter, don't forget a knockout for the air gap.) Depending on the hardware you plan to use, you may need to include larger wooden knockouts for the faucet or air gap's mounting washers and nuts, as described in chapter 2.

POURING THE CONCRETE

To reinforce the concrete, wire together a grid of ⅜-in. rebar on 6-in. centers. (If you don't have any big cantilevers, it's all right to use rebar around the edges of the countertop and remesh in the middle, as discussed in chapter 2.) Rather than hang the rebar from the sides of the form, Al's crew simply placed the grid in the bottom of the form, shoveled in a enough concrete to support the rebar, and then lifted the grid up about 2 in. off the bottom of the form.

Place the remainder of the concrete in the form and move it around carefully by hand. On a piece as thin as this countertop, Al doesn't use a vibrator but simply raps on the sides of the form with a hammer. If you prefer, go ahead and use a palm sander placed against the sides of the form, or wrap the sander in plastic bags, as described in chapter 4, and place it in the wet concrete (and remember, if the bag tears, your sander will be ruined).

While the concrete is still soft, smooth the surface with a wooden darby (a large, wooden float). Check the surface

1. Place the rebar grid in the bottom of the form, and shovel in enough concrete to support it.

2. Lift the grid up about 2 in. off the bottom of the form.

3. Place the remainder of the concrete in the form.

4. Move the concrete around carefully by hand.

▲ To vibrate the concrete, simply rap on the side of the form with a hammer.

▲ While the concrete is still soft, float its surface with a wooden darby.

▲ Check the surface with a 4-ft. level.

periodically with a 4-ft. level. If you want to place any inlays, this is the time to do it, while the concrete is still soft. Place the inlays, then float the surface once again, getting it as flat as possible.

Wait for the concrete's initial set—about 30 min. or perhaps longer—before edging the top of the piece with a ½-in. steel edging tool. Strip away the form, smooth the face of the countertop with a wooden float, and edge the bottom with a ¼-in. edging tool. Smooth the corners with a piece of plastic.

Al's crew proceeded to trowel the surface periodically for the next three

◀ Allow the concrete
to set for about
30 min. and then
edge the top of
the counter with a
steel edging tool.

hours with the fiberglass float, pushing down the rocks and bringing up lots of cream, the mix of fines, cement, and pigments. After that, they went to work on it with steel trowels. "You have to keep troweling until the concrete is rock-hard," Al says. "Otherwise, you don't get a smooth finish." The basics of finishing flatwork (see chapter 4) apply when working on a poured-in-place countertop:

◀ Strip away
the form and
then smooth
the face of the
countertop with
a wooden float.

■ Keep the trowels as flat as possible, at least initially, so you don't dig into the surface.

■ If you get a lot of bleed water on the surface when you trowel, you're working the concrete too much; stop and wait until the surface has lost its sheen, then hit it again.

■ If you see trowel marks when you trowel, it's still too wet.

Every time you take a pass over the concrete with a trowel, you bring up a little more of the highly pigmented cream. Thus every pass tends to darken the surface. Toward the end of

▶ Smooth the corners of the countertop with a piece of plastic.

▶ To ensure a smooth finish, continue troweling the surface periodically until the concrete is hard.

the process, Al troweled some areas more than others to create slight variations in the surface coloring.

If you're going to grind and polish the concrete, of course, then such finishing touches aren't necessary. It is important, though, to get the concrete as flat as possible; otherwise it will be difficult to grind and polish evenly. Follow the steps for grinding, polishing, and sealing as described in chapter 5.

◄ The finished
countertop.

MAINTAINING A CONCRETE COUNTERTOP

Routine maintenance of a concrete countertop is simple. We recommend that you wax your countertop with beeswax or carnuba wax once a month, or at least as often as you do your other furniture. Use a sponge, rag, or nylon pad to wipe up spills as quickly as possible—especially spilled wine, vinegar, and acidic liquids such as lemon or tomato juice.

Do not use cleansers or abrasive pads such as steel wool on a concrete countertop. Though concrete is hard, abrasives will scrape away the protective wax coating and even scratch the concrete.

REFINISHING A COUNTERTOP

If you're not diligent about waxing your countertop and wiping up spills, the countertop will likely take on an increasingly rich patina of stains. We find that these blemishes are not unattractive, but there can come a point when the rich patina becomes, well, a little too rich. Fortunately, stains and other blemishes can be removed with a light polishing, followed by a new application of sealers and wax.

How often you need to do this depends on your tolerance for the less than perfect. My own countertop, for example, went 12 years before I decided it was time for some refinishing. The countertop had been sealed and waxed only once during that time, soon after it was installed. In the years that followed, it was photographed repeatedly and featured in more than 10 magazines, and during that time, no one ever commented on the complex array of stains that covered its surface. We like

▲ ▶ Twelve years of hard use and little maintenance have left this concrete countertop with a rich—or perhaps too-rich—
patina of stains.

to believe that's because the sculptural
qualities of the piece overcame a focus
on the condition of its surface. Still,
the countertop's surface finally reached
the limits of tolerable funkiness, and
I refinished it.

To refinish a countertop:

1. Clean the surface thoroughly with
   mild soap and water.

2. Tape plastic sheets to the edges of
   the countertop to protect the cabinets and floor. Run the tape up past
   the top of the countertop, to catch
   the water used during grinding and
   polishing.

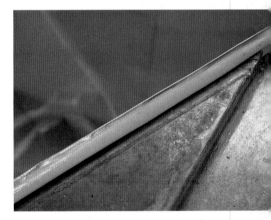

◀ ▲ Before refinishing, tape plastic sheets
to the edges of the countertop.
Run the tape up past the top of the
countertop to keep the water and
mud that's produced by polishing
from dripping down the cabinets
and onto the floor.

3. Polish the surface lightly following the procedures described in chapter 5. For my heavily stained countertop, we started with a 220-grit pad (start with a 400- or 600-grit pad if your countertop isn't similarly covered with the results of a decade's worth of sometimes flamboyant cooking). Polish carefully; you want to remove the least amount of fine surface concrete necessary to remove the stains. We spent about 3½ hr. polishing with the 220-, 600-, 800-, and 1,500-grit pads.

Use a hand pad to polish around inlays, such as brass rods that extend above the countertop's surface, or along the edges of a feature such as an integral drainboard.

4. After polishing, soak up the water and silt with paper towels or rags. Once you've cleaned the surface thoroughly, wipe it down with a clean cloth soaked with denatured alcohol; this will remove any of the fine grit that may remain.

◀ ▲ If your countertop isn't badly stained, start polishing with a 400- or 600-grit pad. If your countertop looks like this one, though, it's probably best to begin with a 220-grit pad, working up to 1,500 grit.

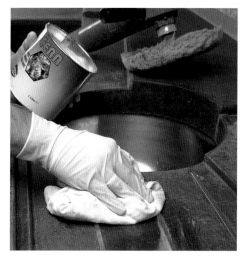

▲ Before and after.

◀ Seal, wax, and then buff the countertop.

5. Let the countertop dry for 10 hr.
   to 24 hr.

6. Seal and wax the surface (see chapter 5 for details), and buff with a car polisher. On my countertop, we used Brightstone penetrating sealer and Monocera beeswax.

RESOURCES

Fabricators and Designers

For the most extensive list of websites and information on fabricators and designers of decorative concrete, go online to: www.Concretenetwork.com

Edgar Cappellin
E.C. Studio
P.O. Box 2141-C
Berkeley, CA 94702
(011-33) 1-4371-7046 (Paris, phone/FAX)
Ecart14@yahoo.com

Fu-Tung Cheng
Cheng Design and Cheng Design Products
2808 San Pablo Ave.
Berkeley, CA 94702
(510) 549-2805, (510) 549-2821 FAX
www.chengdesign.com

Dave Condon
Kilnworks
P.O. Box 2573
Castro Valley, CA 94546
(510) 532-0690

Get Real Surfaces
37 W. 20th St., Ste. 304
New York, NY 10011
(212) 414-1620, (212) 414-1618 FAX

Jeffrey Girard, P.E.
FormWorks
Cary, NC
(919) 434-5339
www.formworks-nc.com

David Hertz
Syndesis, Inc.
2908 Colorado Ave.
Santa Monica, CA 90403
(310) 829-9932, (310) 829-5641 FAX
www.syndesisinc.com

Richard Marks
Concrete Age Artworks
1932 S. Halsted St.
Chicago, IL 60608
(312) 226-3542

Don McPherson
Counter Production
701 Bancroft Way
Berkeley, CA 94710
(510) 843-6916
www.counterproduction.com

Paco Prieto
Pacassa Studios
1793 12th St.
Oakland, CA 94607
(510) 465-4655, (510) 465-9985 FAX
www.pacassa-studios.com

Buddy Rhodes
Buddy Rhodes Studio
2130 Oakdale Ave.
San Francisco, CA 94124
(415) 641-8070
www.buddyrhodes.com

Mark Rogero
Concreteworks Studio
95 Linden St., Unit 3
Oakland, CA 94607
(510) 835-9034
www.concreteworks.com

Steve Rosenblatt
Sonoma Cast Stone
1741 Morningside Mountain Rd.
Glen Ellen, CA 95442
(877) 939-9929
Steve@sonomastone.com
www.sonomastone.com

Soupcan, Inc.
1500 S. Western Ave.
Chicago, IL 60608
(312) 243-6928
www.soupcan.com

Joe Wilson
Arkady Studios
150 N. Mill Creek Rd., Ste. H
Quincy, CA 95971
(800) 930-3323
www.theconcretekitchen.com

General Supplies

Cheng Design Products
2808 San Pablo Ave.
Berkeley, CA 94702
(510) 549-2805
(510) 549-2821 FAX
www.chengdesign.com
Concrete countertop do-it-yourself kits and sup-plies. Complete, ready-to-pour NEO-MIX packaged kits—for amateurs and professionals—that include everything needed to color, pour, grind, and seal countertops. Convenient pre-proportioned pigments, fibers, plasticizers; just add bagged con-crete. Basic kits include a 70-minute instructional video with the author, Fu-Tung Cheng. Full-range diamond grinding pads from 50-grit to 1,500-grit, sealer, wax, water-reducer (plasticizer), fibers, col-ored semi-precious aggregates, and inlays avail-able separately.

K-119 Tools and Equipment
925 San Mateo Ave.
San Bruno, CA 94066
(650) 588-0160
Tools and grinding supplies

Leitch & Co.
1607 Abram Court
San Leandro, CA 94577
(800) 999-8485
www.leitchco.com
Tools and grinding supplies

U.S. Gypsum Industries
125 S. Franklin
Chicago, IL 60606
(800) 621-9622
Durock cementboard

Westside Building Materials
205 S. Linden
South San Francisco, CA 94080
(650) 872-1142
Diamond pads, grinding wheels, sealers, fibers, and tools

Mixers

Imer USA, Inc.
207 Lawrence Ave.
South San Francisco, CA 94080
(650) 872-2200
(800) 275-5463
www.imerusa.com
Reliable, low-cost mixers made in Italy

Mulitquip Corp.
18910 Wilmington Ave.
Carson, CA 90742
(800) 421-1244
Equipment for rent or sale, including barrel mixers up to 12 cu. ft.

Whiteman Industries, Inc.
18910 Wilmington Ave.
Carson, CA 90746
(310) 537-3700
Gas- and electric-powered, towable mixers up to 12 cu. ft.

Sealers and Waxes

Aqua Mix, Inc.
9419 Ann St.
Santa Fe Springs, CA 90670
(800) 366-6877
Penetrating and topical sealers

Brightstone, Inc.
1636 W. 240th St.
Harbor City, CA 90710
(800) 989-5411
www.brightstn.com
Brightstone Universal Stone Sealer

Glaze 'N Seal Co.
18207 E. McDurmott St., Ste. C
Irvine, CA 92614
(800) 486-1414
Water- and solvent-based sealers

Miracle Sealants & Abrasives Co.
12806 Schabarum Ave.
Irwindale, CA 91706
(800) 350-1901
(818) 814-8988 (in Calif.)
511 Impregnator, a penetrating sealer; also grinding and polishing pads

Monocera Beeswax
Industria Chimica General, UC
Via Repubblica di S. Marino
Modena 8-41100
Italy
(059) 450-991/450-978
(059) 450-615 FAX
Beeswax for stone and concrete

NEO-MIX sealer and wax
Cheng Design Products
See General Supplies

Pigments and Stains

Cheng Design Products
See General Supplies

Davis Colors
east:
7101 Muirkirk Rd.
Beltsville, MD 20705
(800) 638-4444
west:
3700 E. Olympic Blvd.
Los Angeles, CA 90023
(800) 356-4848

Fister
2777 Finley Rd.
Downers Grove, IL 60515
(800) 542-7393

Hoover Color Corp.
State Highway 693
2170 Julia Simpkins Rd.
Hiwassee, VA 24347
(540) 980-7233
local distributor:
Pacific Coast Chemicals
2424 Fourth St.
Berkeley, CA 94710
(510) 549-3535

L. M. Scofield Co.
6533 Bandini Blvd.
Los Angeles, CA 90040
(323) 720-3000
www.scofield.com

Pfizer
235 E. 42nd St.
New York, NY 10017
(212) 573-1000

Fibers

Fibermesh
4019 Industry Dr.
Chattanooga, TN 37416
(800) 635-2308
www.fibermesh.com

Hi-Tech Fibers
P.O. Box 469
Edgefield, SC 29824

Plasticisers

Grace Construction Products
62 Whittemore Ave.
Cambridge, MA 02140
(617) 876-1400
Admixtures such as water reducers, sealers, curing supplies, fibers, and other products

Adhesives

Protective Coating Co.
221 S. Third St.
Allentown, PA 18102
(610) 432-3543
Epoxy glues (PC7 and PC11)

3M Do-It-Yourself Division
P. O. Box 33053
St. Paul, MN 55133
Tape and spray adhesives

Rubber Mold Mixing Compounds/ Releases

Polytek
55 Hilton St.
Easton, PA 18042
(610) 559-8620

Smooth-On
2000 St. John St.
Easton, PA 18042
(800) 762-0744

Vibrators

Makita USA, Inc.
14930 Northam St.
La Mirada, CA 90638
(714) 522-8088
(714) 522-8133 FAX
12-volt cordless vibrating poker, model #VR261D

Meadow Burke Products
4555 Airline Dr., #100
Houston, TX 77022
(800) 727-3227
Stinger vibrators

Oztec Concrete Vibrators
65 Channel Dr.
Port Washington, NY 11050
(800) 533-9055
Stinger vibrators

The Wyco Tool Co.
2100 South St.
Racine, WI 53404
(800) 233-9926
Stinger vibrators

Masonry Fasteners

Fas-n-it (formerly: Textron Logistics Co.)
5910 Falcon Rd.
P.O. Box 7033
Rockford, IL 61125-7033
(800) 435-7216
Tapcons

Training and Seminars

Cheng Design Workshops in Creative Concrete
2808 San Pablo Ave.
Berkeley, CA 94702
(510) 549-2805
(510) 549-2821 FAX
www.chengdesign.com
Intensive seminars in concrete countertop fabrication, floors and flatwork, stamping and staining, walls, hearths, and columns—with the best practitioners in their respective fields.

Stainless-Steel Sinks

Elkay Mfg. Co.
2222 Camden Court
Oak Brook, IL 60523
(630) 574-8484

Franke
3050 Campus Dr., Ste. 500
Hatfield, PA 19440
(800) 626-5771
www.franke.com

Just Mfg. Co.
9233 King St.
Franklin Park, IL 60131
(847) 678-5150

Organizations

American Concrete Institute
P. O. Box 9094
Farmington Hills, MI 48333
(248) 848-3700
Provides standards and practices, building-code requirements, software, seminars, and certification

American Laminators Association
P. O. Box 2209
Seattle, WA 98111-2209
(206) 382-1671
Directory of manufacturers

Portland Cement Association
5420 Old Orchard Rd.
Skokie, IL 60077
(847) 966-6200
Technical publications, computer programs, educational materials

www.concretenetwork.com
Comprehensive network site that provides lists and links of concrete fabricators across the country

Books

Concrete Manual
International Conference of Building Officials (November 1998)
5360 Workman Mill Rd.
Whittier, CA 90601
(800) 284-4406, (562) 699-0541
Good, basic text covers everything you need to know about concrete; the book aimed at contractors doing large pours, not the artist or architect

Concrete Structure, Properties, and Materials, by P. Kumar Mehta
(Englewood Cliffs, NJ: Prentice-Hall, Inc., 1986)
The definitive text for engineers, a technical look at concrete, from the molecular level up; if you like lots of technical details, this is the book to have (the craftsman or designer may find it of limited value)

Surface Defects in Concrete
(Addison, IL: Aberdeen Group, 1995)
Covers finishing problems, troubles with architectural surfaces, and prevention and correction of scaling, dusting, bugholes, discoloration, and other flaws

Wabi-Sabi for Artists, Designers, Poets & Philosophers, by Leonard Koren
(Stone Bridge Press, 1994)

World of Concrete Bookstore
Hanley-Wood
426 S. Westgate St.
Addison, IL 60101
(630) 543-0870
(630) 543-3112 FAX
Books on how to make and work with concrete

CREDITS

All photographs © Matt Millman (except where noted).

pp. 2 and 3—photos © Richard Barnes; design and fabrication: Fu-Tung Cheng
p. 4—photos © Robert Ryan
p. 5—photos © Debbie Beacham; builder: Louis Beacham Construction; design and fabrication: Fu-Tung Cheng/Cheng Design
p. 7—design: Banta Architects; fabrication: Kilnworks
pp. 8 (bottom) and 43 (right)—photos © Dave Condon; design and fabrication: Dave Condon, Kilnworks
p. 9 (left)—photo © Bielenberg Assoc.; design: Hok Sport; fabrication: Buddy Rhodes
pp. 9 (right), 10 (center), 12 (top), 15, 17, 23, 27 (top left), 28 (top left, bottom), 30 (top left, top right), 34 (left), 35 (top left), 71, 86 (bottom), and 139 (left)—photos © Fu-Tung Cheng; design and fabrication: Cheng Design
pp. 10 (top), 11 (left), 18, 19 (bottom), 20, 29 (top left), and 174—photos © Richard Barnes; design and fabrication: Cheng Design
pp. 10 (bottom), 27 (bottom), and 33 (bottom left)—photos © J. D. Peterson; design and fabrication: Cheng Design
pp. 12 (bottom), 24 (bottom), 25, 26, 27 (top right), 35 (top right, bottom), 80, and 127—design and fabrication: Cheng Design
pp. 13, 21, 31 (top), 33 (bottom right), and 118—photos © Alan Weintraub/Arcaid; design and fabrication: Cheng Design

pp. 14 and 40 (top)—photos © Edmund Barr; design and fabrication: Josh Chandler
p. 16—photo © Mark Rogero; design and fabrication: Concreteworks Studio
pp. 19 (top left), 32, and 39 (bottom left)—photos © Mark Cohen; design and fabrication: Cheng Design
p. 22—photos © Edgar Cappellin; design and fabrication: Edgar Cappellin
pp. 24 (top), 28 (top right), 43 (left), 86 (top), 93, and 119 (right)—photos © Tom Bonner; design and fabrication: David Hertz, Syndesis
p. 29 (top right)—photo © Don McPherson; design and fabrication: Counter Production
p. 29 (bottom)—design and fabrication: Cheng Design Products
p. 30 (bottom)—photo © Cesar Rubio; design and fabrication: Concreteworks Studio
p. 31 (bottom)—photo © Andre Ramjoue; design and fabrication: Cheng Design
pp. 33 (top) and 146—photos © Scott Paulus; design: VetterDenk Architects; fabrication: Richard Marks, Concrete Age Artworks
p. 34 (right)—design: Phil Banta; fabrication: Kilnworks
pp. 39 (top left, right) and 129—photos © J. D. Peterson; design and fabrication: Pacassa Studios
p. 60—photo © David Fischer
p. 81—photos © Margaret Henry
p. 89 (top)—photo © Bruce Brubaker; design and fabrication: Counter Production

INDEX